Do I to Harm

IDENTIFYING, UNDERSTANDING, AND ADDRESSING MONTHLY MORBID THOUGHTS AND IRRATIONAL BEHAVIORS

BY

CANDACE PEYTON WOFFORD

WAFFLE BAY BOOKS

CORPUS CHRISTI, TX

First Edition: July 2023

First Printing: by Waffle Bay Books

ISBN: 979-8-9887245-0-6

Library of Congress

Control Number: 2023913481

Formatted by: Foysal Rumman

www.fiverr.com/foysalrumman
www.facebook.com/foysal.rumman1

Cover Art by: Maida Y

www.fiverr.com/maida_design

For Jade and PB&J

Table of Contents

Note from the Author:

It is mind-boggling to me that I am writing a self-help book. I have always wanted to be an author, but I used to loathe self-help books, plus I thought I would be writing romance novels. Yes, those books with Fabio on the cover. Have you seen *The Lost City* with Sandra Bullock and Channing Tatum? Love it. Hilarious. I could've, should've, would've been Ms. Bullock's character.

Unfortunately, I cannot, for the life of me, think of the conclusions to my plot lines that I like *"yet"* (… more on that later). Believe you me, I can write romance scenes like nobody's business, but the story? I'm totally stumped. I thought that maybe I needed practice writing, so I started writing articles for an online lifestyle website that features people, places, and events that go on in and around Austin, TX. I was pretty good at it.

All of the articles I wrote received great reviews, which encouraged me to continue writing. I got to interview La French Tech, witness astronaut Thomas Pesquat at SXSW 2023, chronicle changes in education including new tools students could use such as ChatGPT (and the controversy surrounding it) and YouTube's StudyHall. The only thing is, these had nothing to do with romance. I was kind of bummed that my dream of writing fantasy fiction starring two lovers hadn't panned out. Instead, I was on my way to becoming a real-life journalist.

Then came my experience with Premenstrual Dysphoric Disorder (PMDD) and all that comes with it. It took an influencer's Instagram reel and my years of teaching high school freshmen social and emotional learning via trauma-informed practices before I connected the dots. I recorded my symptoms, advocated for myself, and got treatment. Once I was in the recovery stage, I knew that the reason I had been honing my writing skills was to share my story so you too can connect the dots and have the joy and peace you deserve.

Will I ever write romance novels? I hope so. But for now, I need to write this book to save some women's lives. I need to ensure that women have the knowledge to make informed decisions on how to take back their lives so they can be the best versions of themselves. Let's face it, only then would they be able to truly enjoy diving into the pages of adventure and romance.

PART ONE
THE BACKSTORY

Chapter 1:

Recap of my life before becoming a mom

L et's please consider this a conversation, and allow me to give you a bit of my background. I will give you the abridged version; I promise. As you're reading, you may be thinking that my life is not relatable at all, but please don't put the book down because if I can be affected, then anyone can. I am writing this very vulnerable exposé of the past couple of years to save lives - yours, your wife's, your girlfriend's, your sister's, your daughter's, your mom's, your best friend's, and let's be real here; I am trying to save their husbands and children as well. I suffered in silence and was so close to losing it all. I don't want anyone else to go through that, so bear with me while I set the stage.

I grew up in a loving home, with both parents. They are still together after 40 years! I am the eldest of four and all of us were privileged enough to attend private school our whole lives. Our end-of-the-year field trips took us to Paris, Florence, Chicago, Tokyo, Anchorage, and Washington D.C. to name a few. I graduated as the valedictorian and attended the University of Texas... twice. I earned my

Bachelor of Science in Biology and a Master of Science in Marine Science.

As I am writing this, it strikes me just how blessed I am, but I can assure you that I have had hardships and trauma as well. Maybe you can relate to some of those. I've lost many family members who struggled with addiction. I was in an abusive relationship when I was younger. I racked up over $100,000 in student loan debt. I've been passed up for promotions. I've struggled to make ends meet. However, those are all different stories for a different time. Maybe I will write more books about those experiences, but for now, let's focus on the one that, if still unrecognized, would have caused me to lose everything.

While in grad school, I met my husband Jade... at a bar. Bizarrely enough, I had seen him two weeks earlier (ahem, at a different bar... this was grad school in a small touristy beach town mind you so... yeah...). When I saw him that first time, I turned to all my girlfriends, pointed at him, and said, "That will be mine; don't bother even talking to him, ladies, because he is mine." I didn't get to talk to him that night. He left while I was twerking on the dance floor, but two weeks later I saw him again, and that time I did not let him leave without giving him my number. The rest is history.

After grad school, I taught high school for a couple of years, but I was not equipped to handle the students as someone fresh out of college, who did not even go to school to teach. I resigned after 1.5 years when a student overdosed in my classroom during 2nd period on a combo of alcohol and pills. He survived, but it was still a traumatic event for everyone. I left the high school scene but stayed in education and worked at the University of Texas Marine Science Institute for a while before relocating with my husband to California.

We lived in Venice Beach. I got a job working at UCLA's Center for Excellence in Engineering and Diversity. My husband worked in the surf industry. We were living the dream - young married couple, beach, sun, waves, SoCal, glitz and glamor. Then came June 1, 2016. It started as a normal day. I was the first one to the office because I had signed up for the Bruin Health Improvement Plan, which got me to campus super early. The workout bootcamp met at 6:30am and was made up of UCLA employees. It got me in the best shape of my life (ahem, except for high school duh).

Shortly after I arrived at my office, one of my coworkers came in. We had our coffee and chatted a bit until I got a text message from a friend in the finance department: ACTIVE SHOOTER IN YOUR BUILDING. What? My friend and I locked the doors, turned out the lights, and cowered for over three hours, not just *thinking* that we were going to die, but *knowing* that we were going to die. I texted and called Jade, my family, and close friends, telling them that I loved them. I had so much adrenaline running through my body for 180 minutes straight, that now when I see things that used to scare me, they don't bother me at all. Cockroach? Fine. Rat? Bring it on.

We were watching the news on mute on our phones when it was announced that two people had tragically lost their lives. Minutes later we received a Bruin Alert telling us that the lockdown was lifted, and we were free to go. So, we booked it. My friend gave me a ride home because I did not want to wait on the bus, which was my mode of transportation to and from work. My husband was in Texas at the time, so he could not pick me up. One of my aunts thankfully lived nearby and came to get me so I would not have to be alone. When we got to her house, she asked one of her employees to go purchase some adult beverages for me while she started grilling up some Elgin sausage for me so I would have a bit of Texas comfort. I was relieved to not be alone, but still all I wished for was for Jade to hurry up and get back.

He changed his flight to the next one flying out of Corpus Christi and arrived at my Aunt's house to pick me up close to midnight. When we got home, I finally felt safe and allowed myself to cry. I cried myself to sleep that night. The next day, Jade and I decided to try to have a kid. In case one of us ever actually did die, we wanted to have a piece of each other. Eight months later, we were pregnant. My experiences that followed are what led me to write this book.

Chapter 2:

Welcoming our first child

In 2017, my husband and I welcomed our first child, a healthy baby boy. Before we had him, we moved back to Texas to live in Corpus Christi, settling in one week before Hurricane Harvey hit the Texas Coast in August 2017. After many weeks of cleanup and recovery, I started my new job as a high school teacher (again).

Our son was born in early December, and it was one of the colder winters that Texas had in a while. On the fourth day of his life, a day after we got home from the hospital, it snowed… in south Texas… on the beach. We took some quick photos in the snow before heading back inside. My parents had come down to help out but they reminded me after our snowy photo shoot that they had to leave the next day. I was in shock and scared out of my mind, but I put on a brave face and assured them that I would be okay. I mean, I knew how to cook a meal and do laundry. Right? I knew how to balance my time so I would add showers into my schedule without any stress. Right? Ha.

Before I had kids, it was in my mind that my mom would stay with me for a whole month, just like her mom did.

However, my grandmother was a stay-at-home mom, while my mom had a full-time job as a Forensic Toxicologist, and she still had my little brother at home in his senior year of high school. Clearly, I should not have built my hopes up in the first place. The cards were stacked against me. My parents left on day five of our son's life to make it to my brother's state championship football game. It made total sense, but that could not stop me from crying for hours after they drove off. My separation anxiety at that moment, in hindsight, should have been a clue to the fact that my hormones affect me in some crazy ways.

During my whole maternity leave, because of the cold winter, I was stuck inside. Again, thinking back, perhaps that's just how my brain justified me staying in the house all day every day – because it was cold. It wasn't that I was isolating and being antisocial, right?

I went to my OBGYN three weeks after giving birth and explained that I could not stop crying and was so sad and overwhelmed all the time. The littlest changes gave me panic attacks. I struggled to do daily tasks. By daily tasks, I mean cooking, cleaning, and yes, even showering. I used to have long, beautiful, (fake) blonde, wavy hair. After having a kid, I chopped it all off because brushing my hair was a luxury for which I could not find the time.

At my postpartum follow-up appointment, after listening to my complaints, my doctor explained that I could have one of three things, all of which are affected by the adjustment of hormones post-pregnancy: 1) the baby blues,

9

2) postpartum depression, or 3) postpartum psychosis. After talking it out, we determined that it was most likely postpartum depression. I was adamant about not calling it postpartum psychosis because it's not like I wanted to kill my baby; I was just super sad and tired, right? I was most definitely so happy to have him in my life and out of my belly because I hated being pregnant, but I felt so alone because he was no longer physically connected to my body. Explain that line of thinking to me. You can't. Becoming a mom will mess with all of your neurotransmitters, hormones, and chemical pathways, which causes things to not even make sense anymore.

Twelve weeks went by in a flash; or perhaps I should say a blur. I have very few memories from that time period. My brain was in a fog. The sleep deprivation and postpartum depression were real. To me, it felt as if suddenly I was headed back to school to teach, and boy was it rough on so many different levels.

My first day back we went into lockdown because there was a man with a gun across the street from the high school. Are you kidding me? I had already been through this and did not want to go through it again. I took some deep breaths to get it together because I had to be there for my students. That was one of the first times I can remember breathing deeply to calm my body down. The lockdown was lifted within an hour, after it was determined that the man with the gun was not at all related to my campus. He was apprehended and it was back to business as usual.

Ha. Business as usual. Have you ever had to pump breast milk with high school boys walking by in the hallway right outside of your pumping room; I mean storage closet? Don't do it. I had these grand plans to try to make it to one year nursing my firstborn. I stopped pumping after eight months and dried up within ten. Oh well. I learned quickly that I could not dwell on these things. I could not spend time and energy that I didn't have being disappointed in myself for something that was essentially out of my control, and frankly, just wasn't meant to be.

Another challenge was the financial aspect, and I am not talking about costs of diapers and wipes. Our income was totally screwed. In case you are not aware, the way that teachers' salaries are calculated is based on us showing up for all 187 days. Clearly when you are out for 12 weeks, then you do not work 60 of those days. Due to the timing of my leave, once I returned, my remaining paychecks ended up being 1/3 of what I usually earned. It was awful. Struggling through those tiny paychecks added another layer of stress, which meant much more cortisol (stress hormone) was flowing through my body on a daily basis.

One silver lining of the timing of my son's birth was that I only had to go back to work for two months until summer. During that time, my husband took our son to work with him, so they got some major bonding time. Then I was off again for summer, which meant that he did not have to start going to daycare until he was eight months old, which was a blessing to me. By that time, he was sitting up on his own and rocking back and forth in the crawling position so he wasn't as completely helpless as a newborn would be. I was weirded out that other women were going to be holding him and comforting him all day. I wished it could have been me. I never thought that I wanted to be a stay-at-home mom, but Lord knows I wanted to be when it was time for me to start the next school year and him to start daycare. Somehow, we survived.

Cut to a couple of years later. My postpartum depression eventually decreased, and I, for the most part, went back to my joyful self. Jade and I went on dates. I took our little buddy boy to all the fun and cute toddler times that I could find. He was doing great at daycare - learning, playing, and growing. He was talking up a storm and could tell me all about his days at school and who he played with. Then good ol' COVID-19 entered the scene.

Spring Break 2020. Never. Ended. I taught my high school students from home, with buddy boy in the next room. I was nervous because in my opinion he was in this critical period of learning, and I felt as though I would fail him. Enter my middle sister. She had come to visit from L.A. during Spring Break, and because the world shut down, she was stuck and stayed with us for two months. As a BCBA (Board Certified Behavior Analyst) she was completely on point when it came to teaching her favorite nephew age-appropriate curriculum. He was just fine, and I am so grateful that he was at that young age when the pandemic occurred. I'm not sure how we would have fared if he was already in grade school.

Our district stayed virtual through the end of the school year. We were home all day every day. Thankfully, there was no shortage of entertainment - *Tiger King* anyone? Plus, since restaurants were closed to inside dining, Texas finally passed the law allowing alcohol to-go. Coupled with the fact that suddenly memes were everywhere, once buddy boy was asleep at night, let the scrolling and tipsy giggles begin. For us it ended up being a bizarre but fun time.

Chapter 3:

Welcoming our second child

Everyone jokes about how people either got in shape, started a new hobby, or had a baby during the pandemic. Well, that last one was me and Jade. We decided to try to have one more kid before there was too big of a gap between our son and his sibling. We had our daughter in June 2021, and I got to be home during the summer with her.

When we got home from the hospital it was beautiful when we introduced our children to each other. You could tell immediately that our son was going to be the best, most caring, most patient big brother ever. To this day he continues to exemplify all those qualities.

My personal issue when we arrived back home was that I was having a hard time balancing out having two kids and ensuring that one did not feel more (or less) loved and cared for than the other. With our daughter being an infant, the main attention I gave her covered the basic needs to keep her alive. With our son being 3.5 years old, of course we were meeting the basic needs for him, but we also had to concentrate on his emotional needs and cognitive development as well.

It was exhausting. I kept feeling like a failure because I was showing them different amounts and different types of care and probably not meeting one of their needs. How in the world did people raise more than one child? I could not possibly show them the same kind of love when they were at two completely different stages of life and development. These overwhelming feelings led to more crying and more isolation.

Thankfully, my mom got to stay with me for a whole month that summer; she had the days to take off, and my brother was in college at that point, so my parents didn't have schedules and obligations at home to deal with. My mom cooked, cleaned, did laundry, changed diapers, took our son to and from daycare, and brought my daughter to me when I needed to nurse but didn't have the energy to get up.

I was in much more pain this time around. When I had our first, I took the meds for pain but didn't finish the bottle. With my second, I finished the bottle and called for a refill. Was it because I was older? This pregnancy was considered "geriatric". Was it because I had postpartum depression again but leaning more towards postpartum psychosis this time?

My original plan was to return to school in August so that I would work all 187 days to have full paychecks (hello, we were about to have two kids in daycare at $10K/year each). However, when the time came to return to school, I mentally could not do it, so I said I wanted to take seven weeks off. During the extra time at home, I was still ***not*** okay. I thought that the warm months would be better to have a baby because of the sunshine and the ability to go play outside. Instead, I have foggy memories of Jade finding me curled up in a ball on the shower floor, bawling my eyes out, saying that I did not want to be alive anymore.

I hated how I was acting. I hated that I was not being the best mom ever. I hated that I did not understand what was going on with my body and brain. What in the world was happening to me? I love my life. I love my kids. I love my husband. I love our city, our home, and our beaches. Why in the world would I not want to live anymore? It did not make sense to me and yet, that is what my brain was telling me. I extended my maternity leave even more, another five weeks, to take the full time allowed by FMLA.

I got back to school in November and could not handle the pumping again. I stopped nursing when she was five months old. That's also when she started daycare. Things were continuing to look different from when I had my first. Maybe it's because I had a girl, or maybe it's because she was the second child. In any case, I did not realize how bad things would get.

As I returned to work, I attempted to fall into a routine. I started working out again every day after school with my friend, right there in my classroom, as soon as the dismissal bell would ring. I would go home and sit in our backyard while our son played, and his little sister watched him. It was autumn/wintertime, so I would have my seasonal beers that I enjoyed so much. Life on the outside seemed good, normal, but internally, I was struggling and attributed it to postpartum depression, which would eventually balance out. Right? Wrong.

Chapter 4:

Two kids and done

The postpartum depression still had not balanced out by the spring, and Jade and I decided together that it would be best for us to enjoy the two beautiful children that we have, focusing on raising them to be good people, without adding any more tiny humans to the mix.

During Spring Break 2022, I had my tubes tied. I say tied, but nowadays it's more like tubes cauterized. In any case, no more kiddos. People kept questioning my decision to make such a permanent move. They thought I should get on birth control pills or get an IUD in case I changed my mind. I knew I would never change my mind. Being pregnant was hard for me. Being a mother of two was hard for me. I can do hard things, but I want to be the one to choose which "hard" to tackle. Jade and I knew that if I wanted to continue on the path of healing (in my mind I still needed to heal from postpartum depression/psychosis), then I needed to stop after having two kids.

I thought that closing the chapter of having more kids would finally move me toward figuring out who the heck I was. Becoming a mom does some crazy stuff to your brain.

Do I have an identity anymore? Not really. I'm only ever referred to as his mom or her mom. What happened to being called Candace? I used to be cool. I used to be full of joy, full of life. I was the social butterfly. I kept the friend groups together. Want to plan a girls night? Candace is on it. Want to plan a tailgate party? (Hook 'Em, Horns!) Candace is on it. Want to go on a trip with friends or family? You guessed it... Candace will plan the itinerary. Where had that person gone?

Before I lost myself, I was told that my smile brought joy to anyone feeling down. My name 'Candace' means bright, shining light, and I like to think that I did, in fact, shine light on everyone I met. People liked being around me. I was always down for a movie night, Hooks baseball game (minor league affiliate of the Houston Astros), BYOB painting class, Book Club, Happy Hour, a round of golf (mostly to critique, I mean caddy, for my husband), and even the impromptu beach or pool party. Do you think I did any of that in the months following becoming a mom of two? No. No, I did not.

By the next school year (that's how teachers tell time - by the school year calendar), life from the outside looking in still looked great. Jade's career was becoming more and more successful. He started playing more golf and had shared his love with our son, who was a little mini-Jade and loved it too.

Our son was four and already reading. He could tell you states and capitals and find them on a map for you. He also knew the flags of all the countries of the world as well as their geographical location, including countries that I didn't even know existed, let alone knew which continent they were on. He was kind and empathic, and still a great big brother. Our daughter had made it to a year (phew, making it to a year was a goal of mine... why was that my goal? Clearly, I have issues). She was walking, climbing, and talking (babbling) up a storm.

I tried to keep it together. I tried to find joy in things. My entire family (mom, dad, sisters, brother, hubby, and kiddos) went on a wonderful trip to New York together that summer. My cousin was getting married in the Catskill Mountains, and we added some extra days to explore NYC. Our son was totally on board. I mean hello, Mr. Flag Boy loved New York. In the fall another cousin got married. This time in Nashville, TN. What a beautiful city! We booked our family trip and did all of the touristy things and again it was so rewarding to see our kids light up. New core memories were made.

In school, I was finally teaching the subject that I was most passionate about, a class that I helped implement. It's a class dedicated to equipping high schoolers with the tools they need to be the best versions of themselves. My school made it a mandatory one-semester class for freshmen, and it was finally approved for the 2022-23 school year for me to be the lead and teach it every single period!

When people would ask me what I did, my blanket answer was to tell them that I teach students how to manage their emotions… My answer usually elicited a follow-up question asking if I could present a seminar to adults as well. While that does sound like a good idea, I felt that my calling in life was to guide the teenage child during the critical time period when their brains are developing. I wanted to give them the tools to understand how to make rational decisions (using the prefrontal cortex) and not run solely on their emotions and impulsivity (run by the limbic center).

I felt that I was very equipped to teach them this material as my background and master's degree specialized in endocrinology (the study of hormones). Everything that is happening in their bodies is a biochemical or physicochemical reaction, and it helps them when they realize that there are reasons to explain why adolescence can be so difficult. With me, they learned way more than they ever wanted to about their brain, hormones, and hormone receptors.

With that knowledge, teenagers can learn how to check in to make sure that their brains are actually working for them the way they are supposed to be. In the class I gave them the tools for self-awareness, self-management, social awareness, relationship skills, and responsible decision-making. Um. Hello? I am teaching all of this to 14/15/16-year-olds and at the time still hadn't put 2 and 2 together to realize that my own brain was not working the way it should.

During the Fall 2022 semester I struggled to do daily tasks, including the parts of my day that I used to look forward to. It was a chore to feed my family. The old me loved to cook. I watched the Food Network all the time. I requested cookbooks for every birthday and Christmas. I became creative in the kitchen when it came to not only how I prepared the food, but also how I plated it - steaks, grilled chicken, balsamic glazed Brussels sprouts, bacon-wrapped asparagus, peach spiced lamb chops, seasoned kale, butternut squash soup with grilled cheese on rosemary sourdough bread, grilled shrimp, roasted acorn squash with cranberries. If it was colorful and made for a pretty plate presentation, then I was going to make it.

Yet now my kids were surviving on a rotation of chicken nuggets, corn dogs, fish sticks, and pizza. I tried to add mac'n'cheese to the rotation because it's a guilty pleasure of mine, but would you believe that my kids don't like it? I tried different brands - Kraft, Velveeta, Annie's. I tried different shapes - shells, elbow, bowtie, Paw Patrol, Frozen, bunnies. Nothing worked. I guess I should just be glad that their consumption of Yellow Dye No. 5 is lower than it could have been.

I would like to thank the genius who came up with the design for pouches; the ones that have combinations of fruits, veggies, and superfoods blended together. Don't worry. I always bought the blends that included veggies in them, which somehow made it better, since most of the nutrients my kids needed were coming from those pouches.

I had lost my passion for cooking. I no longer read a novel every 3 days. My husband and I weren't watching shows together once we climbed into bed for the night. My house was a wreck. The list goes on.

Did you know that you need gasoline in your vehicle for it to work? Well, apparently, my brain couldn't even manage that. One day I was driving home after picking the kids up from daycare, and I heard a "ding" go off in the car. I could not even fathom what it was about. It wasn't persistent, so I continued my drive home, parked in the driveway, and went inside to plate pouches, cheese sticks, and chicken nuggets. Jade went out to run an errand and when he got in the car it acted like it wouldn't start. When it finally did, he saw that I was below Empty and he coasted to the gas station on fumes. See what I mean about not being able to handle daily tasks?

I was still blaming it on postpartum depression, ignoring the fact that my daughter was over a year old (so really it could not be that, right?). I finally made an appointment with my OBGYN and saw the nurse practitioner. It took her a while for her to pull it out of me, but once she did, I confessed that I had feelings of despair and hopelessness, that I felt like I was floating through a dense fog. She assured me that I was *not* supposed to be feeling that way and attributed it to depression/anxiety. That day I started Zoloft, a selective serotonin reuptake inhibitor (SSRI).

Chapter 5:

Trying to find balance, but still suffering in silence

Things sort of got better... I guess... I could not really tell you because I was still in that fog, detached, and certain aspects of my life were not how I wanted them to be.

I had my dream teaching schedule, yet I left work most days feeling defeated. Here I was trying to teach kids how to be the best versions of themselves and they were still choosing to act like scoundrels (that was the politest word I could think of...). If you are a former student of mine reading this, you know that I love you and care about you. You also know that, oh-my-lanta, most of you tried my patience like it was a full-time job. I still love you though.

On the personal side, my marriage started to have more and more challenges. Jade and I were raised very differently and did not see eye-to-eye on a lot of parenting issues. With two kids it was also harder to find a babysitter, which meant that our date life was almost non-existent. I, once again, felt alone despite having a husband who was totally present for me and the kids. I felt alone, despite having kids who were thriving, and who showed me love all the time with hugs, kisses, artwork, and the words, "I love you".

The fog continued to hover. Recently, I was reminded of just how out of it I was. I took my kids to a bounce house indoor playground and while the kids were playing, a woman, her husband, and their son walked into the play area. My mind did a tiny nudge, thinking that maybe I should recognize the woman, but it was just a fleeting thought, so I did not entertain it for long. Five minutes later, she and her husband walk up and ask, "Oh my gosh is that your daughter?", except they didn't say "your daughter", they said her actual name. They knew her.

They proceeded to remind me that the kids used to attend the same daycare. Jade and I had switched our daughter to go to school with her big bro once she was allowed to attend his school at 18 months, but from 5 to 18 months, she went to school, apparently, with this child. I thought back to those days and started to recall how everyone I saw knew who my baby girl was. The parents of her classmates were always saying goodbye to her, by name, when we would pick up our kids at the same time. The siblings of her classmates loved entertaining her in the window while they were there picking up their little brother or sister, and knew her by name.

I knew no one. I didn't have the effort or bandwidth available to learn the other nine babies' names. I didn't have the brain capacity to even memorize the faces of her classmates, let alone her classmates' parents and siblings. What was wrong with me? How rude is that?

I've always maintained that I have an awful memory. My parents and siblings will talk about something from our childhood, and I will have no recollection of it. My husband often reminds me of fun dates we've been on, but I don't remember them, so I tell him that it was probably when he was dating someone else. He shakes his head a bit and pats me on my shoulder like I'm a child who doesn't know any better, but he doesn't harp on it. I've talked to doctors about my memory (or lack thereof), but they are not worried. They are under the impression that my brain only holds onto information if it's necessary for me to know it for my wellbeing and survival, and it can be perfectly normal for events that did not have a grand impact on my life to be forgotten. Still... meeting those parents again that day was just another reminder that I was coasting through life on fumes (much like my vehicles), barely registering the people, places, and events around me. It made me feel like such a loser that I didn't even take the time or make the effort to be a part of my daughter's preschool experience.

On top of stress from work, a strained marriage, and clearly living in a foggy haze, during September 2022, we were also dealing with health issues with our kids. I was taking one or the other to the doctor every single week, sometimes twice a week, for months. They had fevers, coughs, ear infections, and anything else you can think of that babies and toddlers get! Our son was also losing his hearing. I would talk to him, and he would say, "What?", after everything I said. I was having to repeat myself non-stop, which did not help with the irritability I felt.

I would walk into the living room, and he would be watching TV with the volume on the lowest setting, and I realized that he was just reading the subtitles as he watched. I'd tell him that he could turn it up, but he wouldn't even hear me say that.

I made an appointment with his pediatrician, and she did a hearing test. The results were significantly lower than they were at his 4-year wellness visit. I thought back to my high school years and remembered living in an apartment complex. We were getting sick all the time and my mom finally asked them to do a mold test. Sure enough, the apartment was infested with mold and the parent company of the complex paid for us to live in the DoubleTree Hotel top-floor suite for an entire month while they conducted the mold remediation.

The memory prompted me to get an at-home mold test, and lo and behold, results showed that we had mold. As renters, we were thankfully able to get out of our lease. We searched for houses in our budget and moved across town within 5 days. We had to spend money on deposits, movers, and furniture for our new home because most of the stuff from our old house had mold on it and we did not want to bring it with us. We finally got settled right before the Thanksgiving break. (For those wondering, we did not have to take the kids to the doctor at all once we moved, and our son's hearing has made a full recovery!)

I tell you all this because I want you to realize that I had some major stressors in my life. The presence of these stressors caused me to attribute any anxiety, depression, and feelings of being overwhelmed, to those circumstances, which meant that I had yet to discover and acknowledge the root of my problem. I also wasn't feeling despair all the time anymore, which made me think that I was on the up and up. I still had my days of not functioning, which meant lying in bed, neglecting my motherly duties, and checking out so to speak, but it wasn't 24/7 anymore. Although, when it was bad, it was very bad.

I am reminded of the poem "There was a little girl" by Henry Wadsworth Longfellow:

There was a little girl,

who had a little curl,

Right in the middle of her forehead.

When she was good,

she was very good indeed,

but when she was bad she was horrid.

That. Was. Me. I was rude, impatient, irritable, and irrational, to say the least. The slightest sounds would set me off. One day my hearing was fine, the next, I would swear that I had suddenly developed hyperacusis (a hearing disorder that makes it hard to deal with everyday sounds). I had complete and total sound/noise sensitivity. For me, certain sounds seemed unbearably loud even though people around me didn't have problems with the noise level.

A sensitivity to noise is not something you want to have as a high school teacher. Students would walk in and see my face and ask, "What did 6th period do to you?" or "Are you okay, Miss Waffles?". I could not mask my irritation. In addition to dealing with noise from high schoolers at work, I had young children at home who were probably playing at a normal volume, but I could not handle it. My dad and husband often joke about me, "Momma likes it quiet." It's true. I do. Yet, there were times when I was fine with noises and others when I would clench my fists and jaw before lashing out at people to "SHUT. IT!" What was happening with me?

The days and weeks passed, and we made it to Thanksgiving Break. Thanksgiving has always been my favorite holiday. I love the family, food, fall weather, and football. Of course, we watch the Dallas Cowboys play on Thanksgiving, and we used to watch the Texas Longhorns play on that day too, but a while ago they switched to playing games on Black Friday instead. It bothered me at first, but I have since adjusted my stance on the subject because now it just means that we have consecutive days of football games that I have an interest in.

During the holiday, in between stuffing my face and being a couch potato watching football games, lots of pictures were taken. I did not like what I saw. Why did I not know that I looked like that? I looked puffy and worn down. I still had not lost the baby weight from my daughter. Can it even be called baby weight anymore when the child is 18 months old? In any case, I still had all the weight, despite watching what I ate and continuing to work out every day after school.

After seeing the pictures, I decided to take some action on that front and made a Telemed call asking what they could do to help me lose weight. I mentioned to the doctor that I was on Zoloft for depression, and she said that was the problem: Zoloft has been attributed to weight gain. Ugh. She switched up my meds to a weight-neutral drug, Wellbutrin, which by the way is a Norepinephrine and Dopamine Reuptake Inhibitor (NDRI), which I started towards the end of November.

Chapter 6:

The worst month yet (trigger warning)

Sometime in the beginning of December I was watching a reel of an influencer who I adore. If you are not following @LindseyGurk on Instagram or TikTok, do yourself a favor and go check her out. She is a mom and champion of women. She started a line of clothing, "Get Your Pink Back™" in an effort to help encourage and inspire women. The prints on the clothing are flamingos and designed around the fact that flamingos can lose their pink coloring while raising their children because so much of their food and energy goes to their young. But eventually... they get it back! She encourages her followers to wear the hoodies and remember that while transitional phases are almost always difficult, they can also lead to so much beauty.

One day in her stories, she was sharing very personal things, and I felt as though she was describing me to a T. She said that every month she would find herself in the bathroom on the floor, weeping, feeling like she did not want to do anything anymore, while at the same time wondering why she even thought that because she loved her life.

Hold up. Every month? Was that my experience too? I had to look back and check whether my moments of despair were following a cycle, hello, my menstrual cycle! Yes, I believe that I could say that was the case. Wow. What a revelation. She then went on to name it - PMDD - and shared how she prayed daily for God to release her from her suffering (side note: He did).

Damn. Other women go through what I go through? And there is even a name for it? How had I never heard of this before? I had all the symptoms but didn't know that they were typical of premenstrual dysphoric disorder (PMDD). At that time, I did not tell anybody what I had discovered. I mean, I was still on antidepressants, so I could handle it myself, right? No. No, I could not.

I recall going to a ladies night with friends in December; I just trudged in and sat there the whole night, clearly not functioning. It was almost Christmas, and everyone else was super happy, gearing up for their trips home. There was yummy food, delicious drinks, and we were doing fun holiday crafts. In the past, this would have been my jam. Instead, I just sat there listening to everyone else talk. I rarely contributed to the conversation. If someone said something funny, I would give them a weak smile. When they tried to get me more involved and asked me how things were going with work or family, my response was that I didn't want to talk about it. I ended up being the first to leave. A few called me the next day to check on me, but of course I screened their calls.

A short time later we went to Austin to stay at my parents' house during the week after Christmas. When we stay at their home, Jade and I stay in the guest bedroom where there is also a crib for our daughter to sleep. Our son usually bounces around, staying with his aunts or uncle - one night with one of my sisters, one night with the other sister, and one night with my brother.

I was feeling exhausted and kept taking naps because I finally could (two weeks off during Christmas break when you're a teacher!). I was also very irritable and short with people but would for the most part recognize it and tried to apologize as soon as I snapped at someone. My youngest sister told me later that Jade spoke with her about me, and she tried to have my back and encouraged him to support me and be there for me. But Jade was adamant that there was "something else going on; something is not right". Leave it to the husband to be spot on.

Of course, if he had said anything would I have agreed? Probably not. I would have been hurt and gotten defensive. Mentioning things to a woman suggesting that their behavior could be associated with their period is offensive, right? I mean that's how we've been conditioned to think - that it's an insult to associate behaviors and moods with the menstrual cycle. But in reality, it's a biological and physiological truth.

So somehow, even after learning more and more about the complexities of women's reproductive systems and their brains, when I think about women excusing themselves from certain things because they are on their period, even I still have to stop myself from the knee-jerk reaction of rolling my eyes. I often think about the classic scene in *The Departed* when Leonardo DiCaprio's character orders a cranberry juice and the bartender responds in his thick Boston accent, "What do you got your period?". For my whole life, I've heard jokes about women on their periods and been told that going through your cycle is just something you have to deal with on your own. But is it really? After my experience, I would say that no, that should no longer be the case, for any woman.

One night during that Christmas break, I woke up in the middle of the night from a very graphic nightmare. I dreamed I had murdered my daughter. When I awoke, I want to kill myself. It took me several minutes to realize where I was and that she was sleeping peacefully in her crib, feet away from me. That's the moment I chose to no longer suffer in silence, and to get help.

I hesitated to record in a book that lasts forever what my nightmare was. At first, I was just going to say that the dream involved her and a cast-iron skillet. But then I didn't want people to think that I put her in the oven or something because that would be awful. Wait, what? That's pretty darn hypocritical of me when I'm writing this entire book to empower and encourage women to take a look within, so they can realize that the dark thoughts they are having are intrusive thoughts and means that their brains are not functioning the way they are supposed to, in the hopes that they will get the help they desperately need.

So, who am I to categorize one method of murdering your child as more horrific than another? Anytime a life is cut short, it's tragic. In the nightmare that rocked me to my core, I crushed her with a cast iron skillet; the sound of crunching bones jolted me awake. Am I speaking too brazenly for you on this subject? Perhaps you'd prefer me to tiptoe around it? Tiptoeing implies you want to keep something secret. It implies you don't want to get caught. Well, I do! Catch me! Stop me! These are not the thoughts of Candace Peyton Wofford, so yes, I need to be brazen about it. I need to be "caught".

It still haunts me thinking how close I might have been to infanticide or suicide. The only reason I can write this at all is because I was able to recognize the cycle, the intrusive thoughts, and I have support from my family. I am dedicated to working through the trauma to be the best version of myself. I want that for you, too.

I recently read *Never Finished* by David Goggins. In it, he said that if you have trauma, you should not just be writing about it in a journal but recording it out loud so you can listen to it over and over again until it no longer causes you debilitating pain. Then you will be able to say you went through it and confirm that it did not break you. I have said my nightmare aloud so many times that I am now able to write about it and share it with you in the hopes that you are helped by it, or you can help someone who you think might be suffering in silence.

I could not sleep the rest of that night. Instead, I got on my phone and started researching everything that I could regarding PMDD. I found posts on Instagram that explained what was going on and shared them with my family so they would understand a little bit more about what I was going through. When Jade woke up, I sobbed as I told him about it. When the rest of my family woke up, I started to tell them about it, too.

That day there were even more family functions that I was supposed to attend, but I was so shaken up and full of anxiety about attending them, that I no longer put on a brave face. Instead, I admitted that my brain was going through something, and I was not functioning as myself. My siblings, husband, and kids all went to do the New Year's Day Polar Bear Plunge at Barton Springs, while I stayed home. I was able to finally fall asleep knowing that my dark secret was out, I had the support from my family, and I had a plan.

In my research, I noticed that one of the factors that affects women with PMDD deals with the hormone serotonin. If you recall, the month before I had stopped taking the SSRI and started taking the NDRI. I believe that the horrible symptoms during December 2022 took place because I was no longer on the SSRI. I called my Telemed doctor and made an appointment. When she called me back days later, we talked about my symptoms, the timeline, and the cyclical nature. I told her about the nightmare I had. We discussed PMDD in detail. Her medical advice was to continue taking Wellbutrin, but she also called in a prescription for Prozac (an SSRI) and instructed me to take it the eight to ten days before my period started. The following month, January 2023, I did as she instructed, and it was the best month I had in a long time.

I did not want too many chapters in this book labeled as "trigger warnings", so I would like to include here a few more stories from women I know and admire, who have dealt with some of the same issues of intrusive thoughts and irrational behaviors that I did. I reached out to them, offering to include their stories in my book. I wanted them to write it from their points of view, but only if they thought it would be therapeutic. If it would bring more trauma, then of course I did not want them to contribute. A few of the ladies wanted to give it a try as long as they remained anonymous.

Here are their stories in their own words:

Brave Contributor #1:

During my first pregnancy, I had some problems, but once the baby was born, getting used to life was the biggest challenge. With my second child, however, life was so different. We had just celebrated learning that we were expecting again. It was an exciting time as we had been trying for four years. Now here we were, ready to embark on a new adventure, and our family was growing. As with my first pregnancy, I had issues with bleeding, which made us proceed with caution, but all was going well. I was a therapist in a prominent psychological clinic, and my husband was self-employed.

A month later, however, our lives turned upside down. My husband began to exhibit strange behaviors and limitations. I rushed him to the emergency room, and they treated him like a stroke patient. He had bouts of paralysis that would subside followed by excruciating headaches. Several spinal taps later, they learned he had contracted encephalitis from a mosquito. It is likely that he got bit one night, while outside building a fort for our firstborn. His was the only reported case in Corpus Christi, and the neurologist said that, in his research, he found three encephalitis reports in Florida. My husband remained in the hospital for nine days, and I was losing my mind over the thought of not having my life partner anymore.

When he returned home, my regular nights of insomnia became worse because my husband would wander the house like someone with Alzheimer's. It was frightening. We were in trouble. He had lost his work, after being out for six months, and he had not been released by the doctor to drive. We went to the neurologist every week, and the doctor was impressed with the progress as little by little, my husband's mind improved. He added that the men in Florida had "scrambled eggs for brains" after the infection ran its course. He believed that my husband's situation was a miracle as he showed signs of healing after five months.

My husband's healing continued, and he was able to go on a job interview. I drove him, and he walked back to my office. He got the job. Now we were finally able to enjoy the precious gifts that God had given us, and the baby inside me began to make his presence known. We had a few months of normalcy before I became bedridden and lost my income.

I planned to give birth to my baby without medication. It wasn't because I was trying to prove anything or because I was a strong woman. It was because we had no maternity insurance. We had to pay cash for this one. We made payments every month when I went in for office visits.

When the big day to deliver arrived, I was prepared to push this baby out naturally without medication. Everything was going well until the doctor examined me and said, "This baby is going to be ten pounds. We don't let little mamas naturally have babies this big." I'm not even five feet tall. I immediately asked for the epidural, a $700 dose was on its way, and he was born the natural way.

Everything went well, everything except me. The first month was tough because I had a kidney obstruction when the baby was three weeks old. I was blessed with colleagues from work and family members, who could come and help me. After that, I had four weeks left to work out a routine. I nursed him, but it was painful because he had an underbite and a very strong chomp. At six weeks I had to return to work, so I placed him in a daycare across from my office. I pumped several meals in the evening, nursed him at night, through the night, and in the morning. I took his filled bottles to the daycare and nursed him at lunch time. My body responded to this routine well. Somehow, my breasts learned the routine, and I leaked at work only a few times. I nursed him for seven months.

Although my body was working as it should, my mind was not. I was not sleeping at night even though the baby was. During the day, I was exhausted but still able to meet the needs of those who needed me. It was my thinking that tormented me and the fact that I could not feel happy. I loved my baby and my family. I knew I did, but I could not feel happy. I wore a happy mask every day and tried to say and do things that resembled happiness.

Although I never thought about hurting my baby, I did think about hurting myself. I thought *Would anyone really care if I wasn't here anymore?* I did not have a plan to hurt myself, and although I was a mental health professional, I did not seek assistance right away.

During all this, my periods were out of control. I would soak through a pad every two hours. Tampons didn't work because my flow was so grand, they would just slide out. I was miserable.

My husband and I also noticed some of the behaviors that started before and lingered during my period. I was beginning to think I was bipolar. I had bizarre intense thoughts and ideas. I screamed and threw things. It was not right. Sometimes, he got caught up in the frenzy, too. Eventually, he learned to redirect me by reminding me to take a break or take a nap. Sometimes I became defensive when he did this, but it really did help.

Two things happened that changed me forever. The first was a visual hallucination. I was sitting on the couch watching my two children play, and I began to see things on the floor. I thought they were a couple of black spiders wiggling around on the tan carpeting near my kids. I privately asked my husband to look into it as I did not want to overreact and frighten my children. He looked, and there was nothing there. I took deep breaths because something inside me wanted to burst. I asked him if he could watch the kids. I needed to go outside and clear my mind. He agreed, and I grabbed my rollerblades and quietly hurried outside. I knew if the kids saw me, they would want to come, too. I needed to be alone at that moment. The second event immediately followed. As I was skating along, with no thoughts attached to it, intense anger rose in me. It consumed my chest and head with extreme pressure. This anger came from nowhere. I skated back home and practiced some deep breathing to calm myself down before I went back into the house. I knew there was something very wrong with me.

At that moment, I believed I needed to say something. I needed to tell my husband that I thought I was going crazy. He and I spoke away from the children, and I told him I needed to see someone. Although I worked with an office full of psychologists, I did not feel comfortable telling them what was happening to me. They were my colleagues, and I just didn't want them to know what was going on since I had already burdened them with help during my husband's illness and my medical problems. Instead, I sought help from my medical doctor.

He was able to see me the next day. He put me on Zoloft; it took a week before I started noticing a difference. I was slowly becoming happy again. I finally opened up about my struggles with a few friends at work, and they were very accepting and understanding. I stayed on medication for several years.

Then came my third pregnancy, which had many challenges. The baby tried to come early twice, I was hospitalized to keep him in, and I was bedridden for three weeks at the beginning of the third trimester. My mother suffered a stroke while she was in town taking care of me, and my oldest son was the one who found her. We were able to have her for five more years. My baby was born on time, but one of his kidneys atrophied, and we had to see a specialist for several months. He had reflux that went undiagnosed for three months. Given all this, I was worried that the horrible stress was going to begin an emotional spiral and lead me to the darkness I had previously conquered. This time, I watched for signs. My husband and I communicated frequently about the stress, and I agreed to be forthcoming if the negative thoughts started again.

The best thing I did regarding my psychological, physiological, and emotional struggles was to seek help from my husband, my doctor, and my friends.

Brave Contributor #2:

How do you begin to share a memory that has been so deeply repressed that it's only been uttered aloud once since the incident occurred? In this case I think some background information could be helpful.

I have two amazing daughters who are opposites in every way. These differences apply to the pregnancy, labor, and earlier years of each child's life as well. When we got pregnant with my first daughter, we had been trying for a year, and my husband had just been diagnosed with a rare bone disease. We were told that he would need surgery halfway through my pregnancy and would be on crutches for the first six months of our child's life. He was devastated that he wouldn't be able to walk around holding her or jump up for late night feedings. Luckily, by the grace of God, everything went smoothly. Both the pregnancy and labor were pretty standard. On my 39th week they realized I was leaking amniotic fluid, so I was admitted, and the next morning, I was induced. Eight hours later my beautiful 8.7 pound baby girl was born. Her first couple of years had obstacles, but she was a joy.

When we found out we were pregnant with my youngest daughter, my husband was so excited to be able to experience and participate in everything this time around. However, things got off to a rocky start. This pregnancy was very different and much more difficult. She was sitting very high up and causing a lot of pain. I had to do physical therapy regularly and had a very hard time sleeping. When they said I could again be induced at thirty-nine weeks I was ready.

I was induced at 5:30 in the morning but progressed very slowly this time. She did not want to come out. By 9:30 that evening, I was exhausted and getting quite nervous. She finally did make her appearance, but she was sunny side up causing shoulder dystopia. She weighed almost ten pounds. The doctor did not think that she would be any bigger than 8.9 pounds, so I was never offered a c-section. Needless to say, I was in a lot of pain.

When my other daughter was born, they handed her directly to me, and she latched on right away. That was not the case this time around. They said her cry did not sound right and immediately took her away to the NICU where she spent the first few days of her life. The days that followed were just as hard. She had a lot of stomach issues and cried almost all of the time. We had to order her a special formula that could only be purchased online. Throughout the following year, she was constantly sick and always throwing up or getting respiratory infections. We were stressed and overwhelmed, to say the least.

After about a year and a half she started to get a little better, so we wanted to start trying to live a normal life. We wanted to get out of the house and do things out in nature. One beautiful Saturday morning, we decided to take the boat out. Everyone was super excited and in a great mood. Once we got on the boat, we had to drive at a high speed through the channel. The girls were nervous but excited. Both of my daughters were wearing life vests, and I was holding on to the little one tightly. That's when the first intrusive thought appeared, "I wonder what would happen if I threw her over?" I was completely shocked by the thought. Then came the next. "Go ahead; throw her over. She'll be fine; she's wearing a life vest."

My mind started racing. I couldn't throw her over! What if she hit the water too hard, or what if we couldn't get to her in time? At this point it started to feel like the cliché of a devil on one shoulder and an angel on the other. The scariest part of it all was that the "devil" side didn't seem malicious at all. It sounded calm, logical, even rational. I started to panic as I struggled mentally and physically to fight the growing urge to toss her over. It all became so overwhelming. My head was spinning as the wrong thoughts began to seem as though they made the most sense. I tried to hold my grip tighter and prayed we would reach the shore quickly.

The moment we stopped I handed her over to my husband as fast as I could and got off the boat. I tried to take deep breaths and keep my composure so as not to let anyone find out about the horror that had just taken place in my mind. I felt terrified and guilty. I gathered myself to get through the rest of the "fun" day we had planned (was it even going to be fun anymore?) and convinced myself that it must have just been sleep deprivation. I repressed the thought ever since then, yet it replays in my mind often.

My daughter will be seven years old soon, and I just recently finally opened up about this awful experience. Candace was explaining the symptoms of her PMDD to me, including her irrational behavior and intrusive thoughts, and after our discussion, I felt comfortable enough to speak about this incident for the first time ever. When she later asked me if I thought it might be therapeutic to write about it, my first instinct was to say, "No, absolutely not. How could I admit any of this so publicly?"

However, people say that knowledge is power, and when Candace shared her knowledge with me, it finally allowed me to speak freely about this terrible incident. Once I did, it really felt like a weight had been lifted off my shoulders. Learning from her about other women's experiences helped me realize that I am not alone. I don't know that I have PMDD, but I do know that I suffered through intrusive thoughts after having my second child. I wish I had known then that other women suffer through it, too. I wish I had an outlet at the time to speak up and get help and support. I hope women around the world begin to share their stories, spread awareness, and find comfort and strength in each other.

Chapter 7:
Why this book?

I finally knew what was wrong with me, and I finally had the tools to fix it. My marriage got better. My outlook on my job was healthier. The energy and patience I had for my children was greater. I was finally in a place where I could heal and move forward. But why was it so hard to get to this place? Why did I not know about PMDD before seeing it talked about on Instagram? Why did I end up having to figure it out myself after a horrific and traumatic nightmare? Why do women that I talk to have no clue what it is when I call it PMDD, but as soon as I describe it, they share with me their own experiences with disturbing and debilitating thoughts they've had the days before their period?

Once I figured out what was going on with me, I told everyone. At first, it was difficult, but just as Goggins talked about, it got better every time I shared. The amazing part was that once I shared the nightmare, 1 out of every 3 women would respond, "Well, I have *never* told *anyone* this, but since you told me, I would like to share with you _____".

You read in the previous chapter, in her own words, what happened that day on the boat with my friend. Before speaking to me about it, she had never said it aloud to anyone. She might have gone her whole life without working through the trauma of those intrusive thoughts, while they continued to replay in her head over and over again. Another friend shared that after she had her second child, she recognized that her whole personality changed the days before her period. Her husband would even track the days by looking at her birth control pills, and when the time came close, he opted to take the kids and leave for a getaway because he didn't want them to be around her at that time. He confronted her and told her things had to change before she eventually got help.

Another person close to me deals with PMDD in her 13 year old daughter. My friend knew something was off once her eldest started her period, but she wasn't quite sure what was going on. In the days before her cycle her daughter was depressed and had suicidal ideations. She took her to get help and was brushed off many times before finally being taken seriously and getting the treatment her daughter needed. The young lady is thriving now. The mama bear came out and got it done. My friend did not give up. She was persistent and unwavering in her search for treatment for her daughter. I would like to think that most mothers would be like this. So why are some of us not persistent and unwavering when it comes to our own treatment?

The previously mentioned scenarios are just a couple of the stories that have been shared with me. They might make you uncomfortable, but the truly appalling aspect is that in each of the instances, something in their bodies was not working properly. Except for the young lady with the mama bear, the shame from the thoughts and behaviors (that weren't even from their own true selves, mind you) prevented them from getting help as soon as they noticed something was not right.

I loathe watching the news. Can't stand it. Don't want to know. So it's disturbing that when I'm scrolling through Facebook, a news story will be there front and center about a woman who killed her children. Everyone interviewed always says the same thing - that this came out of nowhere and that they never suspected that anything was wrong. To that I would argue that it most likely did not come out of nowhere. You don't just kill your precious children unless there are some major mental issues going on. I would argue that if you looked at their menstrual cycles, 1 in 20 would be days from starting their period and in the throes of PMDD. It doesn't excuse what happened, but damn, it does show that if they had gotten the help they needed, then the tragedies might have been avoided. It took a nightmare for me to get help, and it often crosses my mind, "What if I never did?".

One day in class, during a lesson on recognizing and managing emotions, I was telling my students that they first must figure out what it is that they are feeling before they can address what's going on in order to make sure that their brains get back to working the way they are supposed to for them. The School-Connect® curriculum I used teaches, "If you can state it, you can regulate it; If you can name it, you can tame it". It struck me at that moment, that women don't know what the heck is going on with their brains, hormones, receptors, genes, and chemical pathways, and they don't even have the name PMDD associated with it, to be able to state it or name it. As the saying goes, "You don't know, what you don't know", and for some reason, people do not know about PMDD. That is why I decided to write this book.

Chapter 8:
A brief history of PMDD

I've been writing specifically on how Premenstrual Dysphoric Disorder started for me after I became a mother, but you should know that PMDD can begin anytime during a woman's reproductive years. People may think that it is a bad case of PMS that happens only sometimes. They would be wrong. PMDD is a very severe form of premenstrual syndrome (PMS) that occurs every single month and affects the way your brain works.

During the late luteal phase of most menstrual cycles (hello, the days before your period starts), women tend to experience cramping, bloating, and headaches. In addition to the physical symptoms, women who have PMDD experience anger, irritability, feeling overwhelmed, anxiety and panic attacks, difficulty concentrating, depression, and even homicidal and suicidal thoughts. The debilitating emotional and mood-related symptoms impact life and relationships.

Severe menstrual symptoms have been recorded since ancient times. In *Mind and Madness in Ancient Greece: The Classical Roots of Modern Psychiatry* by Bennett Simon, he notes that Hippocrates (who lived in the 5th century BCE) described women who had suicidal thoughts prior to the onset of menstruation. After many more records and thousands of years passed, the syndrome was recognized in the 1930s in *Archives of Neurology and Psychiatry* as premenstrual tension syndrome before the more common term premenstrual syndrome (PMS) was adopted in the 1950s.

It would take another three decades before late luteal phase dysphoric disorder (LLPDD) was described in 1987 in the appendix of the *Diagnostic and Statistical Manual of Mental Disorders, Third Edition, Revised (DSM-III-R)*. A few more years passed before it was recognized formally in 1993 as a mood disorder and named as premenstrual dysphoric disorder (PMDD) in the *Diagnostic and Statistical Manual of Mental Disorders, Fourth Edition (DSM-IV) Source Book Appendix*.

In 1998, a panel of 16 psychiatry experts from the U.S. and abroad gathered to review the evidence and take a vote. From the meeting, it was determined that PMDD should no longer be categorized as a mood disorder, but instead, a clinical disorder. However, it would not be until 2012, in the *Diagnostic and Statistical Manual of Mental Disorders, Fifth Edition (DSM-5)*, that PMDD would finally be recognized as a distinct disorder by the American Psychiatric Association. The criteria for PMDD are listed in the manual of *mental* disorders (*not* in a manual detailing obstetrics or gynecology), and lay emphasis on the timing, nature, and severity of symptoms. Finally, it wasn't until 2022 that PMDD was recognized world-wide in the

International Classification of Diseases 11th Revision (ICD-11).

Jean Endicott explained the process of diagnosing PMDD in her article "History, Evolution, and Diagnosis of Premenstrual Dysphoric Disorder" found in the *Journal of Clinical Psychiatry*:

- There must be at least 1 year's duration of symptoms that occur during the days before menstruation.

- At least 5 or more of the 11 specified symptoms (listed below) must be present.

- At least 1 of the 4 dysphoric mood changes must be present to a marked degree of severity.

- There must be evidence of psychosocial impairment in that the condition must seriously interfere with their work, social activities, or interpersonal relationships.

- Criteria must be confirmed by prospective daily ratings during at least 2 consecutive symptomatic cycles.

The DSM-5 states that one or more of the following symptoms must be present:

1. Markedly depressed mood, feelings of hopelessness, or self-deprecating thoughts.

2. Marked anxiety, tension, feelings of being "keyed up" or "on edge".

3. Marked affective lability (e.g., mood swings, feeling suddenly sad or tearful, or increased sensitivity to rejection).

4. Marked irritability or anger or increased interpersonal conflicts.

The DSM-5 adds that one (or more) of the following symptoms must also be present, to reach a total of five symptoms when combined with the symptoms from the above criteria:

5. Decreased interest in usual activities (e.g., work, school, friends, hobbies).

6. Subjective difficulty in concentration.

7. Lethargy, easy fatigability, or marked lack of energy.

8. Marked change in appetite; overeating; or specific food cravings.

9. Hypersomnia or insomnia.

10. A sense of being overwhelmed or out of control.

11. Physical symptoms such as breast tenderness or swelling, joint or muscle pain, a sensation of "bloating", or weight gain.

Continued from Endicott, below are ways to distinguish between PMDD and other Depressive Disorders:

- Mood disturbances are cyclical, tightly linked to phases of menstrual cycle with predictable onset and offset.

- Hormonal replacement therapy can provoke cyclical dysphoric mood changes in women with a history of PMDD.

- Symptom stability is seen across cycles.

- Cyclical occurrence of symptoms ceases during pregnancy and postmenopause.

- Prevention or suppression of cycling gonadal hormones relieves symptoms.

- Most common chief complaint is irritability.

- Physical symptoms of PMDD are unique (e.g., breast tenderness and bloating are most common).

- The genetic and environmental risk factors for premenstrual-related symptoms and lifetime major depression are not closely related.

- PMDD is more likely to respond to serotonergic antidepressants than to other antidepressants.

- Upon treatment, symptom improvement is rapid (within the first treatment cycle) and intermittent dosing is effective.

- Upon treatment cessation, symptoms return rapidly and reemergence is more predictable.

Yikes. How are you doing? I'm not quite finished so stay with me. A 2017 *Harvard Health Blog* explained in the article "Premenstrual dysphoria disorder: It's biology, not a behavior choice" that women with PMDD suffer from an increased sensitivity to reproductive hormones during the luteal phase. This leads to alterations in the brain chemicals and neurological pathways that control mood and the general sense of well-being. Furthermore, researchers at the National Institutes of Health (NIH) found that women with PMDD have an altered gene complex that processes the body's response to hormones and stressors.

In the 2017 *Current Psychiatry* article "The etiology of premenstrual dysphoric disorder: 5 interwoven pieces", Dr. Edwin R. Raffi and Dr. Marlene P. Freeman explain that the involvement of genetics means an underlying neurobiological pathophysiology is in place. Thus far, research includes studies of the estrogen receptor alpha (ESR1) gene, serotonin gene polymorphism, serotonin transporter promoter gene (5-HTTLPR), seasonal affective disorder (SAD), and methylenetetrahydrofolate reductase (MTHFR) gene. Hoffman *et al.* reported significant effects for MTF2, PHF19 and SIRT1 genes in the 2017 *Molecular Psychiatry* article, "The ESC/E(Z) complex, an effector of response to ovarian steroids, manifests an intrinsic difference in cells from women with premenstrual dysphoric disorder."

The above paragraph is a mouthful, and understanding the complexities of the genes and their expression takes expert knowledge. I am so grateful that more research studies are finally being conducted, because women have been suffering through PMDD for a long time and we are ready for answers. The most current article I found was published in April 2023 by Stiernman *et al.* In the study, subjects with PMDD were compared to control subjects who were asymptomatic. They both underwent functional magnetic resonance imaging (fMRI) during different phases of the menstrual cycle, while brain responses to emotional stimuli were measured. The images were then related to serum levels of ovarian steroids, the neurosteroids allopregnanolone (ALLO), isoallopregnanolone (ISO), and their ratio ISO/ALLO. As you can imagine, there were differences. Women with PMDD showed altered emotion-induced brain responses in the late-luteal phase, which they concluded may be related to an abnormal response to physiological levels of neurosteroids.

When we learn to talk about PMDD more often, awareness and research regarding reproductive psychiatry will increase. This is dependent on women coming forward with their issues. Once that happens, more of us can participate in studies to multiply the knowledge base. It will help to understand why women with PMDD, compared to women without, have differences in the genes that process the sex hormones estrogen and progesterone. Furthermore, women's lives will be positively affected when we know what treatment options are best and how to make those readily available.

By the way, despite my background in biology and reproductive endocrinology, this chapter was hard for me to write. I felt flustered, foolish, and frankly embarrassed that I did not know almost any of it, which meant that my future readers most likely didn't know it either. This information is knowledge people need. These are the answers to the question of why I was having such a hard time functioning as a human being: my brain and body were not working the way they should. Now it was time to fix it.

PART TWO
THE FUTURE STORY

Chapter 9:

Now you know... so what?

Hopefully you realize that you are not alone. Hopefully you realize that you are not a bad person even if you've had monthly disturbing thoughts and irrational behaviors. Hopefully you realize that you are worthy of a beautiful life, and you should not have to suffer in silence anymore.

The National Institutes of Health estimates that 4.4% of U.S. adults experience bipolar disorder. The World Health Organization states that schizophrenia affects 1 in 222 adults; that is 0.45%. These percentages are less than those affected by PMDD (estimated at 5%), yet we've heard the names of these diseases, and most of us could explain them to a certain degree.

The only reason we don't know about PMDD is because many of the symptoms result in such horrific feelings and behaviors that we are too embarrassed to reach out. For some reason, we think that those feelings are actually ours (they aren't) or that perhaps our irritable behavior is due to the other people's attitudes (it's not), and we really aren't acting that badly (we are).

Dr. Mary T. Jacobson, chief medical director at Alpha Medical is on board with making sure women, health care providers, and society at large take PMDD seriously. She notes, "We often assign harmful and limiting words to conditions like PMDD and PMS, such as emotional, dramatic, moody, hysterical, acting crazy—when women and girls experiencing these conditions are enduring truly severe symptoms that affect them in extreme ways, all from hormone shifts that cause a central nervous system response that they cannot control. From both medical and cultural standpoints, we need to better validate this condition and educate women about how to recognize it, and get the support they need."

Once you lift the lens of shame and look at what is happening from a completely objective point of view, then you will have the courage to speak about it. Once you name it, you can tame it. Once you state it, you can regulate it. Women with PMDD have some pretty dark thoughts, myself included. When that happens, it's because our brains are no longer working for us. We know it can function the way it should because for 20 or so other days out of the month, we are fine. It's those eight to ten days before our cycle that everything changes. Obviously, there is something going on in our nervous and endocrine systems. So talk about it!

Once you have found the courage to admit that there might be something off with your brain, hormones, receptors, or chemical pathways, then you can start the process of healing. The Harvard Blog encourages women to do the following: track your symptoms, educate yourself, reach out to peer support groups, start with lifestyle changes, and talk to your doctor.

Tracking your symptoms might feel daunting at first but remember that this data is needed for your doctor to analyze and could help you find the best treatment. As you research, consider looking at The Johns Hopkins Reproductive Mental Health Center or The Massachusetts General Hospital Center for Women's Mental Health. I live in Texas and found that Baylor College of Medicine has a very reputable Reproductive Psychiatry team. Their website has loads of information for you to start learning more about this disorder you didn't realize existed. Depending on where you live, you may have another fabulous source of help right near you. Be proactive and start to research.

I've shared with you how the use of SSRIs helps me get through those eight to ten days. As someone who studied hormones, receptors, and their coupled chemical pathways, I think medicine is fascinating, and I am glad I found something that works for me. I know not everyone wants to take medicine, and I will share plenty of other options with you in the following pages, but I have to ask, because I did some good ol' WebMD research:

- Do you take Ibuprofen? "Ibuprofen works on one of the chemical pathways for pain. It reduces the ability of your body to make prostaglandins — chemicals that promote pain, inflammation, and fever. With fewer prostaglandins in your body, fever eases, and pain and inflammation is reduced."

- Do you take cough medicine? "Guaifenesin belongs to a class of drugs known as expectorants. It works by thinning and loosening mucus in the airways, clearing congestion, and making breathing easier. Dextromethorphan belongs to a class of drugs known as cough suppressants. It acts on a part of the brain (cough center) to reduce the urge to cough."

- Have you ever been on birth control pills? "Hormones in birth control pills prevent pregnancy by stopping or reducing ovulation (the release of an egg from an ovary), thickening cervical mucus to keep sperm from entering the uterus, and thinning the lining of the uterus so that a fertilized egg is less likely to attach."

If you're okay with taking a pain reliever, cough suppressant, and/or birth control, why wouldn't you be okay taking a selective serotonin reuptake inhibitor or other medication that has been developed to specifically address your issues? If you are willing to take the SSRI or try another form of treatment, keep advocating for yourself until you find which one works for you. I started out on Zoloft. It didn't fix my problem. I switched to Prozac for the ten days before my period, and I am a functioning human being again.

I want you to realize that it's important to do what you need to do not only for your physical health, but for your mental health, too. And let's be realistic here, or as my sisters say "LBRH": your mental health IS your physical health because it's addressing issues with your brain and chemicals, which are physical things!

Despite the research on PMDD not being exhaustive by any stretch of the imagination, I can tell you that there is not a one-size-fits-all treatment. You should be trying to figure out what works and doesn't work for you, because PMDD is a chronic condition that *does* need treatment. Consider the following options that Johns Hopkins suggests:

- Changes in diet to increase protein and carbohydrates and decrease sugar, salt, caffeine, and alcohol

- Regular exercise

- Stress management

- Vitamin supplements (such as vitamin B6, calcium, and magnesium)

- Anti-inflammatory medicines

- Selective serotonin reuptake inhibitors (SSRI)

- Birth control pills

This list may not have the answer for you and your circumstances. If you start to research, join PMDD support groups, and follow PMDD experts (even on social media), you will learn that women are trying lots of things to help and they will share with you what worked and didn't work. Treatment can include any combination of vitamins, supplements, lifestyle changes, SSRIs, therapy, cycle suppression, chemical menopause, or surgical menopause.

The International Association for Premenstrual Disorders (IAPMD) is a great resource. It has links to trials and studies, video support groups, their YouTube channel with lots of information, treatment options, research, symptom tracking, events and webinars, and podcasts just to name a few. IAPMD also manages Facebook support groups you could join including IAPMD - PMDD Moms Support Group and IAPMD - PMDD, Oophorectomy, Hysterectomy, & Life After Group, both of which are private.

I joined both groups and have been uplifted by the love, compassion, and support from the women in the group and I know you would be too. Plus, you could learn about ways other women are coping with the PMDD thoughts and behaviors. I can't even count the number of times I've read posts from women swearing by acupuncture and antihistamines. Who knew a tiny needle or tiny allergy pill could help someone with PMDD? Our bodies are incredible, and there is hope that you can get your mind and body to work the way it should. Keep searching until you find what works for you.

If you are a mother struggling with PMDD, join a group that talks specifically towards parenting with this disorder. If your PMDD is preventing you from keeping a job and having a career, find a group that addresses this issue. *See Her Thrive* is made up of leading menstrual health and menopause experts who are committed to creating inclusive and supportive workplaces where everyone can thrive. Register for one of their workshops or attend an event to make connections with others like you. There is a huge community out there. Let's make sure everyone knows about it.

Chapter 10:
The power of thought

If we want to be champions for all women, we need to start with ourselves. In case you didn't know, men make more money than women on average. It was presumed that it's because men are better negotiators. However, studies have shown that women are the better negotiators, but only when it comes to negotiating for someone else. Women make some of the best agents because they fight for their clients to get the best contracts, best deals, best signing bonuses, and the best perks from the company.

The same is true when it comes to lifting other people's moods. If our friend is down, we do everything in our power to cheer them up. If they are dreading going to work, school, or a specific function, we pump them up, and encourage them to go and have a fantastic time. Why don't we do this for ourselves? Why don't we talk positively to our own brains to pump ourselves up?

In the class I teach, the School-Connect® curriculum includes a lesson on the Power of Thought Loop. The concept is that our thoughts lead to emotions, emotions result in a behavior, and the behavior has an impact on our life. I will give you the example of a negative power of thought loop that I give my students. Let's say you start at a new high school in the middle of the year, and you walk into the cafeteria and think, "This is going to suck." Your emotion is that you feel nervous. The behavior is that you end up sitting by yourself. The impact is that you don't meet any new people, and you feel lonely. The next day, you do and feel the same way and the cycle repeats itself.

Here's an example of the positive thought loop: you start at a new high school in the middle of the year, and you walk into the cafeteria and think, "I don't know anyone, but I will find someone friendly." Your emotion is that you feel hopeful. The behavior is that you sit with a group of people. The impact is that you enjoy talking with them and feel happier. The next day you do and feel the same way and the cycle repeats itself.

Remember when I mentioned Goggins saying that you should record yourself voicing the trauma you went through, listen to it over and over again, and eventually you will be able to say it didn't break you? The same goes for your mood. He says that when you get up in the morning and you are dreading all of the things, record yourself on the microphone. When you play it back, you will most likely cringe listening to the complaining and whining voice coming out of the speaker. He says to record a second take, this time with you pumping yourself up to tackle all of the things you're dreading that day. Then listen to it.

He doesn't call it the power of thought loop, but that's what it is. You have to stop that negative thought loop in its tracks. You have to condition your brain to recognize it, and flip the script to a positive power of thought loop. You need to start pumping yourself up. You need to start lifting yourself up. No more beating yourself up because you have these thoughts and behaviors. Call it what it is, stop wondering what is wrong, start to make the changes to get your brain to its healthiest, and keep moving forward.

When it comes to your mind, you have the control to adjust your thought loop. But what about those intrusive thoughts – the awful ones that almost seem like part of your subconscious? There are many different types of intrusive thoughts that can run through your brain, but here are seven that you might be aware of:

1. The thought of hurting a baby or child.

2. Thoughts of doing something violent or illegal.

3. Thoughts that cause doubt.

4. Unexpected reminders about painful past events.

5. Worries about catching germs or a serious illness.

6. Concerns about doing something embarrassing.

7. Intrusive sexual thoughts.

Take a look at number one again. GoodRx Health reports that nearly half of all new parents have this thought run through their minds. HALF. They go on to talk about postpartum depression and mention that nearly 70% of new moms with PPD envision something bad happening to their child, and 50% of those new moms envision that they are the ones who cause harm to their child. You. Are. Not. Alone. You just need to recognize the cycle, see that there are times that your brain is not working for you, seek the right people to help you, and carry out the action items you both come up with as part of your treatment.

When it comes to intrusive thoughts, Harvard Medical Publishing advises to:

1. *Identify the thought as intrusive.* "Think to yourself, 'that's just an intrusive thought; it's not how I think, it's not what I believe, and it's not what I want to do.'"

2. *Don't fight with it.* When you have an intrusive thought, just accept it. "Don't try to make it go away." Fall back to number one and repeat it over and over again until you are able to move forward.

3. *Don't judge yourself.* Know that having a strange or disturbing thought doesn't indicate that something is wrong with you.

They go on to say that you can, "See a mental health professional if unwanted thoughts are starting to disrupt your daily life, particularly if they're impairing your ability to work or to do things you enjoy. However, even if intrusive thoughts aren't affecting your life in a significant way, you can still see someone to get help." My thoughts were affecting my life in a significant way. I was spiraling out of control. I had to deal with my thoughts to get better. I want that for you too.

I read something posted on FaceBook the other day. It said, "This is why children are 800% worse when their mothers are around: Because YOU, mama, are their safe place. YOU are the place they can come to with all of their problems. If you can't make something better, then who else can? YOU, dear mama, are a garbage disposal of unpleasant feelings and emotions. If a child's been holding it together all day, in an unpleasant situation, the second they see you, they know it's time they can finally let go."

Seven months ago, that was not me. My kids did not gravitate towards me. They always chose Jade over me. They wanted him to take them places, him to read them books, him to make their snacks, him to lay with them. I was out. Dad was in. How messed up is that? Of course, it is not messed up that my children love their dad; the messed up part is that they could not trust me to be there for them in the way they needed me to be. That should have been another clue. If my kids can sense something is wrong with me, then why am I not taking note of that and doing something about it? Why do I keep lying to myself that everything is fine?

One day I got home and my son said, "Are you sad again, Mom?" Damn. That's rough. Out of the mouths of babes, right? That same night, I put my daughter down, and she was crying within one minute. I went back in and rocked her, this time singing a nice little song, laid her back down, and she was up crying again in two minutes. Jade goes in, and she is asleep within 10 seconds. Damn.

That awful Christmas break with the nightmare, I was getting ready to bathe my son, and I was getting frustrated that he was lollygagging. I was so irritable that all of a sudden I was crying again. He ran out of the bathroom to get Jade, my mom, my dad, anyone who would listen. My mom told me that he came to the kitchen and said, "Mom is sad again." Needless to say, I was relieved of bath duty that night.

We tried sleep training for a period of time. That didn't last long. I would get so frustrated with our son when he would not stay in bed that we would end up yelling at each other. Jade would have to break it up... a fight... between a 37 year old woman and 4 year old boy. I had a very small window of stress tolerance and would go from zero to 100 in seconds flat. The irritability I felt towards the nighttime routine was unreal.

Does any of this sound familiar to you? Then something is not right. Do not wait until it is too late or even almost too late to talk to someone about it. Speak up now! Your friends need you. Your kids need you. Your partner needs you. And you need to be living your life without the added trauma of the symptoms of PMDD! It's time to figure out how to deal with your thoughts.

Chapter 11:

Recognizing when you are dysregulated

I keep telling you that your brain should be working for you. It helps to understand what exactly that would look like. Allow me to break it down for you like I do my students. This will be in simple terms; I am not a neurologist after all, but I do have a pretty good understanding of the basic parts of your brain and what their functions are.

First we have the brain stem, which is in charge of basic bodily functions. Evolutionarily speaking, this was the first part to evolve, and is referred to as the bottom or reptilian or hindbrain. The brain stem takes care of all things you don't even have to think about - breathing, blinking, digesting food, and your heart beating just to name a few. The brain stem has been working your whole life, in fact it worked when you were in your mother's womb. You did not have to tell it to start working.

The same is true for the limbic system, or midbrain. This part of your brain triggers emotion (anger, sadness, fear, excitement) and releases hormones that signal pleasure, relaxation, or stress. To make it even simpler, I refer to these as the "happy" hormones such as dopamine, serotonin, and oxytocin, or the "stress" and "anger" hormones such as adrenaline and cortisol. This part has also been working your whole life. Have you ever heard a baby cry or witnessed a toddler throwing a temper tantrum? Exactly… meaning that even since we were infants, we've had experience using the limbic system.

The highest part of your brain is the prefrontal cortex, which is your rational center, also known as the forebrain. It helps you with rational thought, problem-solving, and *managing* your emotions. This part of your brain does not develop until you reach high school. As a teacher, there is no way you could get me to teach 8th graders. I just won't do it. I don't have the patience. But I'm fine with freshmen. Why? Because their prefrontal cortex works and they now have the ability to manage their emotions… At least, that's the way it's supposed to work. Lord knows some of them don't do that. I'm sure you can think of more than a handful of adults who don't manage their emotions either. The point is, biologically speaking, they could, and that's what I teach them about in class.

When the body gets stressed or anxious, the limbic system is alerted to a potential threat, and the five senses are heightened while the body goes into flight, fight, or freeze mode. The hypothalamus triggers the adrenal glands to release adrenaline and cortisol. When these hormones start coursing through the bloodstream, the heart beats faster, lungs breathe harder, blood vessels dilate to accommodate the extra blood flow, pupils dilate, and skin sweats.

These reactions are part of the stress response designed to help us survive, as in survive an attack from a bear or mountain lion. This is the only way our body knows how to respond, which means this is the way it responds when we are walking to the front of the room to give a huge presentation at work, paying a large amount down on a credit card bill, or arguing with the ol' husband.

Not that I have ever argued with my husband. Yeah right, of course I have. This book is about being honest with myself and others, right? Of course, Jade and I have argued. However, since teaching social and emotional learning and the science of the brain, I have been able to recognize when I am going from a regulated state to a dysregulated state. When I recognize it, I am able to take the proper precautions to bring myself back into a state of regulation so I don't end up saying or doing things that I will regret.

The best method that works for me is to take a step away from the situation. I say, "Jade, I am totally dysregulated and about to say or do something that I will regret so give me a minute." I begin to take deep breaths and go to another room or even outside. When you take deep breaths, it activates your parasympathetic nervous system, which slows the release of cortisol and induces the release of oxytocin and serotonin. Suddenly, you are back in control.

Getting your brain back to a regulated state even causes your functional IQ to increase. Ever notice that when you are pissed off you can't even think of the words you want to say? That's because when you are dysregulated you are in a reactive and emotional state, working from a bottom-up brain, which means the prefrontal cortex is not involved at all. As a teacher, I can tell you that when kids are dysregulated (let's say they got in a fight with their boyfriend or girlfriend during the five-minute passing time), they will not do well on the test I'm giving. The same reasoning is true for adults: when we are dysregulated, we are not in the right state of mind.

I mentioned to you before about how I stop myself from continuing to fight and be awful to Jade when we are in a fight...that's nice... Do you think I do that every single time? Nope. I've been too far gone many times to stop myself, and it most certainly happened more often than not during the time living with PMDD and not treating it.

I told you our marriage suffered, and we started marriage counseling. Well. I would attribute the reasoning for us beginning counseling to my behaviors and the subsequent ones from him. Thankfully we found someone who had worked with PMDD before. My mother-in-law watched the kids while we went to a therapist's home in the evenings, and we would sit on her huge, comfy leather couch in front of a roaring fireplace. During the sessions, not only did she help me, but she also helped Jade understand PMDD a little bit more and how he could more efficiently support me in my healing journey. Now, thank God, we are in a joyful and healthy place. The days before my period, we can call it what it is, and I am extra mindful to monitor my mood changes and my intrusive thoughts. You can do that too.

If there are other people close to you being affected by your intrusive thoughts and irrational behaviors, then maybe it's time you shared with them what's going on. For me, that meant talking to my 5 year old son. I explained to him that sometimes I have days when I cannot handle the stress load and will take a lot of breaks. He also knows that there are times when noises are way too loud and my fuse is very short. He can sense when noises start to bother me by noticing the tension in my face and neck. He will disappear for a moment and return with two earplugs for me. We don't even have to address it every time anymore. He just knows and we are in a good place now that I have a coping mechanism in place with the earplugs. You can get yourself to a good place too. Start the hard conversations so you can have people in your corner helping you.

Chapter 12:

Managing your emotions

T here are many different strategies you can use to regulate yourself. The key is finding the one that works best for you. Some are simple; some require a bit for planning, but all of them have the same results of managing your response to the stresses, conflicts, and disappointments of life.

Removing yourself from the situation is a great way to take a time out and gives you a chance to cool off in a place with physical distance from the situation. I suggested to my students that they use this method the next time they were in an argument with their parents. Most responded, "Oh hell no, my mom would kick my ass if I walked away from her in the middle of a fight."

Um. Hello? Did I ever tell them to turn their backs on their parents and walk away? Nope. I told them to call it what it is, say that they are dysregulated, and respectfully ask for a brief respite for them to calm down before they did or said something that could turn their one-week grounding into a one-month grounding. The students still maintained that it wouldn't work, even though I had already told their parents about the strategy in an email, so I'm inclined to not believe some of those students when they say it won't work. But you can only lead a horse to water, right?

Their opposition to using this strategy did bring up a valid point, though. If the person you are having a disagreement with does not understand this concept of regulated versus dysregulated, then they could, in fact, take offense to you wanting to stop in the middle of an argument to have a time-out to cool off. This is just another example of *you don't know what you don't know*. The term "dysregulated" should be in every single person's vocabulary. I am sharing it with you, and you can share it with the people in your lives. Let's spread the word about PMDD *and* dysregulation.

Another way to manage your emotions is to exercise, which releases the natural chemicals (endorphins) that help you let go of tension to feel better. This fact always reminds me of Reese Witherspoon in *Legally Blonde* when her character Elle Woods says, "Exercise gives you endorphins. Endorphins make you happy. Happy people just don't shoot their husbands. They just don't." I'm not sure it's that simple, but I do know that every time I work out, even if I had been dreading it, I leave the gym feeling renewed and ready to *carpe diem* - seize the day.

People often suggest journaling to deal with stress. Writing it out can help you get some distance while you think things through and review your progress. On the flip side of the coin, you could talk it out with someone, which helps you connect with others while you attempt to understand the source of the issue. On the same side of that coin, you could talk it out to yourself, like Goggins suggested. Record your thoughts and play them back to see what you sound like. Do you agree with what you're thinking, or are you totally off base? In either case, you're taking that extra step to examine the situation when you record and listen to your thoughts.

Deep breathing is another strategy and one that I use daily. I start every single class with breathing. I have a Hoberman sphere that I open and close, which mirrors the breaths that the students and I take. It's a method you can use that takes your mind off the stressors and puts it on your breath. This also gets more oxygen to your brain, which allows the neurons (brain cells) to have the reactant it needs for cellular respiration.

Cellular respiration takes place in every single one of your trillions of cells inside the "mighty mitochondria". (Are you having Biology flashbacks yet?) Let me explain. It takes in the oxygen that you breathe and the food that you eat and converts those into the products carbon dioxide and water, which are waste products that you breathe out, sweat, or urinate out. That's just part of the story. The important component is that adenosine triphosphate (ATP) is made. ATP is your energy source. Just like fossil fuels have to be refined into gasoline for your cars to use, the reactants you take in have to be refined into ATP for your cells to use. When you breathe deeply, it supplies an influx of the oxygen needed for cellular respiration. When your cells have enough ATP, they can function the way they are supposed to.

Just like you need oxygen for the reaction, you also need glucose. Glucose is a simple carbohydrate (a sugar) that is found in the food we eat. Have you heard the term "hangry" before? It's a combination of the words hungry and angry. Sometimes, if we go too long without food, we become irritable. This response is because our brain is no longer functioning properly, and part of that can be attributed to the fact that you have lower energy due to lower ATP production. This means that simply eating something can often be a way to get your brain back into a state of regulation.

The Snickers campaign was definitely onto something when they said, "Hungry? Why wait?" in their 90's campaign. They revamped it during the 2010 SuperBowl halftime show commercial starring Betty White, which featured the new slogan, "You're not you when you're hungry". This concept of hunger triggering irritability is widely known, but people don't associate the word dysregulated to the situation. It's time that changed.

Finally, I would like to mention mindfulness as a strategy to regulate yourself. This practice has been around forever, but I did not learn more about it, much less put it into practice, until I took a mindfulness class for employees that was part of a mental health awareness push at UCLA. Every Tuesday and Thursday for 12 weeks we met on campus in a yoga studio at the gym and practiced mindfulness. I learned how to breathe, clear my head of thoughts, and focus on the present. It was an amazing class, and each day I left with more peace of mind.

The Mayo Clinic says, "Mindfulness takes place when you focus on being intensely aware of what you're sensing and feeling in the moment, without interpretation or judgment. Practicing mindfulness involves breathing methods, guided imagery, and other practices to relax the body and mind and help reduce stress." This is different from meditation in that there is no religious component to it. You are merely training your brain to focus on the present moment, which results in a calm demeanor, a quality found in those who manage their emotions well.

These are the main strategies that I teach, but my students have contributed many more suggestions to the list, which means that what I have proposed is just the tip of the iceberg. Things my high schoolers do to manage their emotions include listening to music, zoning out to one of their favorite shows, working on puzzles, coloring, building Legos, baking, knitting, and reading books.

A group I follow on Instagram recently posted reminders for the PMDD parent. They advised to educate your family (even your children in an age-appropriate manner - just like me with my son, noise, and earplugs), plan ahead if you can predict when your symptoms will start, practice patience and forgiveness, fill your own cup first (hard for moms in general!), find treatment that works for you, find your coping mechanisms, and practice consistency.

If you don't already have a go-to method for regulating, you need to get one, or two, or three. Your livelihood depends on it. Take back control of your brain (and life) and have your strategies in place.

Chapter 13:
Carol Dweck's Power of Yet

The idea of taking back control might seem scary to you. "What if it doesn't work?" "This is impossible." "There is something wrong with me, and I can't fix it." Those are thoughts of someone with a fixed mindset, not a growth mindset.

A fixed mindset believes that abilities are fixed from birth and limited, and that there is little opportunity for change and improvement. Unfortunately, the fixed mindset can be seen all around us with people saying things like, "She's a born leader", "She's a chip off the old block", "He's a natural", and "Like father, like son." This way of thinking takes away your control. It means that whatever you try to do, it won't help. That is not a way to live.

Instead, I urge you to have a growth mindset. With a growth mindset, you believe you can do anything you set your mind to with time, effort, and practice, and that opportunities are limitless. People with growth mindsets say things like, "Life is what you make of it", "If you believe it, you can achieve it", and "If at first you don't succeed, try, try again."

Do you have a fixed mindset? If so, you should do things to combat that. Challenge yourself by embracing things you're not naturally good at. Learn from your setbacks and use the knowledge you learned to fuel your comeback. Debate your thoughts by changing your "can't" into "can't, YET".

The *power of yet* comes from researcher Carol Dweck. She studies the brain and how people function when they add that little word "yet." A school she worked with stopped giving failing grades, and instead, if a student did not learn the concept, the report card said, "not yet". The performance of the students increased significantly after that. Another school had the lowest performing kids in the region when it came to state tests. One year, all of the teachers and administrators got on board with making sure the children added the word "yet" to their statements, and by the end of the year, they were outperforming everyone else on the state exams. The addition of this three letter word can change your mindset from fixed to growth.

In my house, no one is allowed to say that they can't do something. They have to add "yet". The rules apply to our kids as well. Our son will be super frustrated with a game on his tablet or Nintendo switch and shout out, "I can't do this", and we will say, "Can't what?", to which he begrudgingly responds, "Can't yet!".

The power of yet can be applied to anything and everything - math abilities, reading/writing skills, public speaking, athletic abilities, social skills, artistic skills, theater skills, and employability skills. Teach it to your friends, partners, kids, everyone. Make sure you practice adding YET to your vocabulary as well because it can be used with regard to your PMDD:

★ "I haven't built up the courage to get help, YET."

★ "I don't understand what's going on in my brain, YET."

★ "The strategies I'm using to regulate myself don't work, YET."

★ "I haven't gotten control of my PMDD, YET."

★ "I haven't bounced back from this setback, YET."

★ "My friends and family haven't seen the best version of me, YET."

Chapter 14:

Bouncing back from setbacks

Having a growth mindset is how you bounce back from setbacks. Crappy things are going to happen in life, but it is not what happens to you; it's 1000% how you respond to it that matters. This is being resilient.

re·sil·ient

adjective

> 1. (of a person or animal) able to withstand or recover quickly from difficult conditions.

In class we do a project on "famous failures". Students have to research a person who has overcome adversity and persevered. Many of the "failures" they get to choose from are very popular, but I only allow two students to a famous failure, so they have to quickly pick who they will research before someone else does. Favorites include Albert Einstein (failed high school math), Michael Jordan (didn't make the Varsity basketball team his junior year), J.K. Rowling (*Harry Potter* author was rejected 12 times before finally being published), Henry Ford (failed five times before his company succeeded), Lizzo (lived out of her car as she battled depression and felt as if she had no purpose after her father's death), and the Rock (cut from the NFL after only one day). They research the person and find out their failure, how they overcame it, and what the person says about the experience. You're starting to get the point of the assignment, right?

Can you guess who was charged with sabotage and attempting to violently overthrow the government, which landed him 27 years in prison? This person got out of prison and became the President of South Africa. He was instrumental in bringing an end to apartheid in South Africa and won the Nobel Peace Prize for his efforts. That's right, Nelson Mandela.

Do you know who the Jewish Austrian psychiatrist was, who was in a concentration camp during the Holocaust? This person lived through physical and mental torture in the camps, all while grieving his brother, mother, and wife who were murdered by Nazis. After surviving, he wrote *Man's Search for Meaning*. This would be Viktor Frankl, who believed that even in the most dire circumstances, we have a choice over our attitude and our ability to find meaning in life.

Mandela and Frankl are posterchild examples of bouncing back from setbacks and overcoming obstacles. Furthermore, you could say they never would have been diagnosed with "victimitis". The suffix *-itis* is used in pathological terms that denote inflammation and hence, abnormal states or conditions, excesses, tendencies, and obsessions. When you connect it to the word victim, I'm sure you know where I am going with this.

Many people believe they are the victims in life, that they have no control over their lives, and that everyone and everything is out to get them. The harsh reality is that when you have this type of thinking of you always being the victim, it is very hard to change your life since you've essentially given the power over to everyone and everything else.

If you want to be able to bounce back from PMDD, then you can't stay angry over the fact that you have it. Instead, start to figure out how to make it better. Find your people. Find the ones who you can open up to and tell them what you are feeling. Just the simple act of not suffering in silence will lift a great burden off of your shoulders, and will put you on the path to healing. Don't give PMDD one more day of controlling your emotions and behaviors.

William Ernest Henley wrote the poem "Invictus". Read it below to remind you: **You are the master of your fate, you are the captain of your soul.** Here is the full poem below, one that Nelson Mandela read every day during his imprisonment.

"Invictus"

By William Ernest Henley

Out of the night that covers me,

Black as the pit from pole to pole,

I thank whatever gods may be

For my unconquerable soul.

In the fell clutch of circumstance

I have not winced nor cried aloud

Under the bludgeonings of chance

My head is bloody, but unbowed.

Beyond this place of wrath and tears

Looms but the Horror of the shade,

And yet the menace of the years

Finds and shall find me unafraid.

It matters not how strait the gate,

How charged with punishments the scroll.

I am the master of my fate.

I am the captain of my soul.

Chapter 15:

Being the best version of yourself

Every day is a new day. Yesterday is over, and there is nothing we can do to change it. Tomorrow may never come. All we have is today. We should spend it being the best versions of ourselves. It's easy to regret the things we've done while out of our minds. It's easy to be pissed off that we're the ones suffering from PMDD when our friends and family members aren't. It's easy to finally be able to excuse some of our thoughts and behaviors once we realize our brains aren't working for us.

It's hard to admit that we are not being the wife /friend /mother /sister /daughter or even person we are supposed to be. It's hard to divulge to our loved ones what's been going through our heads. It's hard to acknowledge we have a problem and need help to fix it. It's even harder to continue to live like nothing is going on or thinking that nothing can be done about it. Choose your hard.

I chose to take a look within and did not like what I saw. I really didn't like the fact that I was no longer the person my husband and kids needed me to be or even the person who I wanted to be. I was no longer functioning as the teacher my students needed me to be. I was no longer checking in on my friends like I should have been. All of that happened because my brain was not functioning the way it should.

I now acknowledge my PMDD and have taken steps to address it. I can still get more irritable than usual in the days before my cycle, but I name it to tame it and state it to regulate it. I take my deep breaths and instead of getting totally exasperated with my husband and kids, I can label what I am feeling as not my own, breathe, and keep moving forward.

Not every day is rainbows and cookies and roses. Some days I'm still in the trenches. However, I am able to get out of those trenches with the knowledge of what's happening in my body and with the love and support of my people. Your people are the ones who bring out the best in you. They are the ones who encourage you to be the best version of yourself. Have you seen *As Good As It Gets* with Jack Nicholson and Helen Hunt? He tells her, "You make me want to be a better man."

Who or what does that for you? Your husband? Your kids? Your friends? Your pets? Your beliefs? Your current plans? Your future? Find your people. Find what makes you want to be the best version of yourself. Keep those in the forefront of your mind.

I encourage you to notice the important people in your life, and see if you are able to celebrate their achievements much more than before when you weren't thinking clearly. *Mudita* is a term used for sympathetic joy, which occurs when you get joy from other people's success. Don't let self-pity, jealousy, envy, or victimitis chase away your sympathetic joy (also known as positive empathy).

Just like learning to regulate yourself, practicing sympathetic joy is a habit you can establish with some mental exercise. Jeremy Adam Smith, author of *The Gratitude Project: How the Science of Thankfulness Can Rewire Our Brains for Resilience, Optimism, and the Greater Good*, suggests eight exercises to get better at practicing positive empathy:

1. Watch a competition without taking sides.

2. Capitalize on positive events.

3. Try to ease envy.

4. Write a self-compassionate letter.

5. Try loving-kindness meditation.

6. Try the common humanity meditation.

7. Try meeting someone's gaze.

8. Let someone do something nice for you.

Studies show that when we have positive empathy, our brain activates the reward center, we have greater feelings of life satisfaction and happiness, better personal relationships, and overall greater well-being. Who wouldn't want all of that?

I was suffering from premenstrual dysphoric disorder, but it took an influencer's Instagram and my years teaching of high school freshmen social and emotional learning via trauma-informed practices before I connected the dots. I hope I have helped you connect the dots too. It's time to love yourself enough to forgive yourself and move forward. Love yourself enough to regulate yourself. Love yourself enough to use the power of yet. Love yourself enough to bounce back from setbacks without playing the victim. You deserve to live a life full of peace, joy, and fulfillment. That won't happen when your brain isn't working the way it's supposed to. Take the steps to get your brain to work for you, not against you. Only then can you be the best version of yourself, celebrate others when they succeed, and even enjoy curling up with an adventurous romance novel or two.

Chapter 16:
A Call to Action

I told you about the IAPMD FaceBook groups that I joined. Guess what. These nationwide groups each only have around 7,000 members. My Corpus Christi Mamas FaceBook group has over 10,000 women in it. A weight loss support FaceBook group that I joined has over 200,000 members. There is something not right with these numbers.

As of July 31, 2021, according to the *US Census Bureau*, there were 95.92 million women between the ages 10-54 (remember PMDD can affect any woman of reproductive age, so that includes the women who have gone through puberty all the way through until they go through menopause). Again, holding to the 5% statistic, that means there are 4.8 million women in the United States who suffer from PMDD, which is exponentially greater than the mere 7,000 women who heard about and joined the FaceBook support groups. The problem is awareness. It's time to make sure everyone is aware that this is a real diagnosis that affects millions of women.

To look at it another way, for every 20 women you know, 1 of them has PMDD. I used to teach at a high school that had 140 female teachers. I know that I have PMDD, but that means that 6 more of my colleagues also suffered from it. Who even knows if they knew what was going on with their bodies and minds during a specific time period every month? I want everyone to know what this is. A disorder that affects millions of women should no longer be unknown, nor should it be so difficult to diagnose. The awareness has to spread like wildfire if we want to save lives as well as the livelihood of those women and their loved ones.

I chose the title of my book for a variety of reasons. On the one hand, it is because I want the women, themselves, to *Do No Harm*. I wanted to share my experiences so women could potentially understand what is going on with their minds and bodies in order to get the help and treatment they need to stop doing harm; harm to themselves, their work life, home life, relationships, attitude, behaviors, the list could go on and on.

On the other hand, *Do No Harm* also applies to everyone else with whom we interact. I want all the medical professionals who are supposed to be helping people with their problems to know how to respond appropriately. When we go to our doctors for help, they should know about the disorder and how to treat it. If, God forbid, a woman commits a crime while in the throes of PMDD, the courts should know about it and how to include in the sentence mandates for her to be able to address her mental health.

When our work life is negatively affected, I want all the bosses and people of Human Resources to understand how to respond to the condition and work with their employees to come up with practical and feasible solutions so women can continue to work. (Side note: In February 2023, Spain became the first European country to approve premenstrual leave, making it only the sixth country in the world to do so after Zambia, Japan, Indonesia, Taiwan, and South Korea.) I want the husbands, children, and friends to learn what it means so they can have ways to respond that will make the family stronger. Everyone could benefit from understanding PMDD.

The calls to action came about as I continued to do research on what happens when PMDD is left untreated. I am sure there are many more "letters", as I call them, of departments, organizations, and people who could benefit from the knowledge, but these professions that follow were heavy on my heart, which is why they are included here.

As a woman, you may be tempted to talk to your OBGYN about what has been going through your mind. But as I was researching PMDD, I read horror stories about mothers confiding in their OBGYN only to be reported to Child Protective Services (CPS) and lose their children for months at a time. Wait, what? You go to the doctor's office begging for help, and their only recourse is to take your kids away from you, saying that you are an unfit mother? Unfortunately, this happens because there is a strong disconnect between psychiatry and obstetrics.

To become a gynecologist or obstetrician, you do not have to take any courses or do any residency training in reproductive psychiatry; they can get their degree to practice without knowing anything about changes to a woman's mind once she has reached reproductive age. The doctors conducting annual exams and delivering babies have very little information regarding what's going on when their patients come to them with feelings of anxiety, despair, or depression. Furthermore, when a patient who is a mother starts telling doctors about ideas that they have had on harming themselves or their children, they do their due diligence as mandatory reporters, and CPS gets involved, which often can cause even more trauma.

Contrastingly, if you were to speak with a psychiatrist about your thoughts or an endocrinologist about your behaviors, then they would recognize the ideas for what they are - intrusive thoughts - and the behaviors would be recognized as a result of pattern changes in hormones and how they are processed. You could then develop a game plan for you to overcome them. You would not go to a dermatologist if you sprained your ankle. Likewise, you should not be going to a general practitioner or lady doctor for issues that are actually of the mind.

Thankfully I found help through my telehealth doctor. I wonder if I had gone to my OBGYN if he would have reported me to CPS if I told him about my dream. I trusted him to take care of me and deliver my child, but could I trust that he would know what to do if he had knowledge of my thoughts?

The U.S. officially recognized PMDD in 2012. It was officially recognized internationally in 2022. This is brand new stuff. My doctor who delivered my son had been practicing medicine for 40 years, which means he never took a course that explained PMDD. My doctor who delivered my daughter had been practicing for 15 years, which makes me think that he didn't take that type of course either.

If women don't even know about PMDD, but are going to their OBGYN doctors for help (because they think they are women issues, not brain issues), then it would be in the best interest of the patient for the doctor to have taken a reproductive psychiatry course. I envision a future where that happens.

I mentioned Hippocrates earlier, how he recorded instances of women who had suicidal thoughts before their cycle. It's fitting that I mention him again here via the Hippocratic Oath. When people finish medical school and become doctors, they take an oath. Part of the oath includes *Primum non nocere*, a Latin phrase that means "first, do no harm". If all OBGYNs were trained in being able to recognize the symptoms and signs of PMDD, along with an understanding of all the treatment options available, women who go to them asking for help would be getting the answers they need, which would hopefully correspond to no harm being done.

Eventually, I would like *all* doctors to know and understand what PMDD is, at least as much to be able to refer their patients to the right person. There are many women who go to their GP or PCP for help and the doctors they speak to downplay what's going on. I have heard stories of doctors replying with, "Back in my day that was called PMS" or "Oh that's just PMS; my wife gets that" or "I see in your charts you have PMDD; is that what we are calling PMS now?". The patient continues to try to advocate for herself, explaining that PMDD is new in the *DSM-5* and *ICD-11*, but the doctor is adamant that it is "just PMS and it will pass".

Having a medical doctor downplay what we're feeling is not helpful. Women have told me that they hate going to the doctor because of how he or she makes them feel. They leave feeling worse off than when they arrived because the doctor talks to them like they are crazy or annoying. That is not acceptable. Please help me, yourself, and all women by continuing to have the tough conversations. You should not have to jump through hoops to figure out what is going on in your brain and body. Neither should the next woman. Let's continue to pave the way.

Let's revisit the scenarios when someone is reported to Child Protective Services and a case worker or social worker is sent out to the house to investigate. If they show up during the 20 days of sunshine, they may not see anything wrong. If they show up during the 8 days of the luteal phase, also known as "hell week", they are more than likely going to witness at least some irritability, but may or may not mark it down as such. What if people in the CPS and social work field were also trained in asking questions that could help one recognize PMDD?

As I read more about PMDD, analytics would of course force more awful news stories to pop up on my feed about women harming their loved ones. For a number of the cases, OBGYNs and CPS or social workers had already been involved, so the warning signs were there, and yet, the women did not get the support and treatment they needed, so ultimately someone was harmed. This has to stop. If women are wanting help, then we need to be able to direct them to the right place. For those who weren't helped, oftentimes horrific things happened, whether it was to their own self or to someone they love.

I am not saying that every woman who has committed a crime has PMDD, but I am saying that for those cases when the behavior seemed to come from nowhere, it is a distinct possibility. There are even some court cases that have used PMS and PMDD in the criminal defense of mothers. Christine Ro, in her 2019 *BBC* article "The overlooked condition that can trigger extreme behaviour", reviewed some of the better known cases in the UK, US, and India that used the defense:

- London, UK. 1981. Sandie Craddock. Her charge was reduced from murder to manslaughter.

- Virginia, USA. 1991. Geraldine Richter acquitted of drunk driving.

- Rajasthan, India. 2018. Woman acquitted of murdering one child and harming the other two.

No one should evade the consequences of the crimes committed. The courts still need to dispense justice accordingly. However, if people of the courts understood the intricacies of PMDD, then perhaps the accused could finally get the treatment she needs, whether that treatment happens inside or out of the walls of prison.

To take it a step further, imagine you have committed a crime, were found guilty, and had to serve time in a women's prison. Imagine that you have PMDD, but you don't know it. Imagine being incarcerated with the other 168,448 women in jail, state prison, or federal prison in the United States (numbers as of December 31, 2022. *Prisoners Series (1980-2021)*. Washington, DC.). Now recall that when women are together for lengthy periods of time, they will begin to menstruate at the same time... Yup. If we are sticking with the data that suggests 5% of women suffer from PMDD, and if we assume that all of those women are of reproductive age, then you and your closest 8,421 friends across the nation are all experiencing the disturbing and debilitating thoughts and behaviors, in a confined space, once a month, every month, for the duration of your sentence.

The 2016 Women's Health Magazine article by Kristina Marusic, "The Sickening Truth About What It's Like to Get Your Period in Prison: A look into the cruel and disturbing ways female prisoners must deal with their menstrual health", exposed how many women in prison don't have the access to feminine hygiene products during their cycle. Furthermore, the physical symptoms of the menstrual cycle, including pain from cramps, would be addressed only if you had money in the commissary to buy acetaminophen. Knowing that, do you think the psychiatric symptoms of the phases of the menstrual cycle are being addressed for women in the prison system, especially when those women may not even know what is going on themselves? I think not.

Let's bring it back to the general population. Women's medicine as a whole is not where it should be. The access to *healthcare* that actually *cares* for and addresses your *health*, is lacking. Did you know that women were left out of clinical trials until the 90s, as in the 1990s? That's right. It wasn't until 1993 that Congress passed the National Institutes of Health (NIH) Revitalization Act that called for more women and minorities to participate in federally-funded clinical trials. It has been 30 years since the law passed. The attention to women's health issues has definitely improved over the past three decades, but there is still a long way to go before we reach gender equality in research.

Furthermore, there are now links between low socioeconomic status and negative psychological health outcomes as well as a lack of information and resources found among women of color who need mental health care. Despite the Revitalization Act, data is still skewed considering women of low SES and women of color do not report their thoughts, behaviors, and symptoms. Our healthcare system needs to address this. The mental health of all women needs to be advocated for and awareness of

PMDD needs to spread to reach all communities and populations.

Empathy is when you see what someone else is going through, imagine yourself in their shoes, and feel what they are feeling. It's hard to feel empathy for something you know nothing about. This call to action is for all of those who care about women. I wrote this to spread the word. I wrote this to educate people. I wrote this so the women who are suffering once every month to function at work, home, and in their relationships learn about something that might be the cause. I wrote this so they can take back their lives. I wrote this to ensure that women get the help they need before it becomes too late. Help me help you. Help me help others. In the words of Kevin Hart, "Help me. Help. Me." We can change the narrative to make sure that the term PMDD is recognized, understood, and given the attention it deserves.

Chapter 17:

When the outlook looks dim, try the Up look

I wanted to publish this book days ago but felt as though there was still a piece missing. I thought about it, asked my friends and family for advice, and prayed about it. My faith is a part of me, so I knew that I just needed to trust God to show me what I needed to do. It all came together in one weekend, shortly following my prayers for help.

On Saturday, June 24, 2023, I made my early morning cup of coffee in my favorite Christmas mug, which, yes, stays out all year round. I mixed the Gevalia Columbia coffee with International Delight Cinnamon Churro Creamer and added an extra dash of cinnamon. I cannot stand lukewarm coffee, but I also don't want to burn the top layer of my tongue off. The amount of creamer I add brings my cup of coffee to the perfect temperature.

I sat on my couch and opened up the YouVersion Bible app on my phone. My kids, who usually wake up at 5:30 in the morning (insert facepalm), were still asleep at 6:15am (insert party hat) so I got to read the entire Verse of the Day and corresponding Devotional in one sitting. The verse was Psalms 42:11.

Psalms 42:11 (NIV)

Why, my soul, are you downcast?

Why so disturbed within me?

Put your hope in God,

for I will yet praise him,

my Savior and my God.

The June 24, 2023 Devotional was titled "Songs in the Dark". It explained how even in the most challenging moments, God is with us and hears us. When we are feeling so hopeless and helpless, we end up being completely honest with God. We share our raw feelings because we have no filter to hold them back.

Psalm 42 is a lament psalm, expressing deep sorrow, written by someone who cannot even explain why he is depressed. Holy cannoli. That sounds like something I have done while lying on my bathroom floor weeping. It sounds like what Mrs. Gurk described in her reel, the one that taught me the term PMDD in the first place. I know from my IAPMD FaceBook support groups that many of the women cry out with laments and pleas for help.

After reading the devotional, I felt like God wanted me to include it in the book, so other women would know that it's okay to have these feelings and question why this is happening to them. However, I still wasn't totally convinced how/why to add it… yet.

The next day, after my morning coffee routine, which was uninterrupted for the second day in a row, thank you very much, the whole family piled into the car for the 8:30 am Sunday morning service. We attend Church Unlimited with Pastor Bil Cornelius in Corpus Christi, TX, and during our time attending that Church, Jade and I have grown in our faith and our marriage. I have also heard God speak to me multiple times while at church, so I have a real sense of peace when we attend. That morning, June 25, 2023, the message that was preached helped me realize what I needed in my book.

The pastor explained the differences between a calling and an assignment. Your calling doesn't change; it lasts your whole life. Assignments do change, and they have timelines, deadlines, and usually someone who holds you accountable to go along with it.

I believe that my calling is to educate, whether it's at the K-12 level, University level, Women (ahem, current book), parents of teenagers (ahem, 2nd book in the works), or teenagers themselves (ahem, you get it, third book). That Sunday morning, I knew that God had made it an assignment for me to include the verse, the devotional message, and how my faith helps me through my tough times in this book.

My hope is that you realize that your songs of lament are valid and Someone is listening. You are not alone. For me, I have to remember to actually speak to God. I have to remember verses of the Bible like "The Lord hears his people when they call to Him for help. He rescues them from all their troubles. The Lord is close to the brokenhearted; he rescues those whose spirits are crushed" *(Psalms 34:17-18 NIV)* and "I consider that our present sufferings are not worth comparing with the glory that will be revealed in us" *(Romans 8:18 NIV)*. I have to listen to "More Than Able" (by Elevation Worship, featuring Chandler Moore and Tiffany Hudson). These are my go-to methods to gain peace of mind during the hard times. What are your go-to methods?

For everyone who made it to this last chapter, you should be proud of yourselves for taking the first step and acknowledging that there might be an issue. Bravo to you. Please don't stop there. I encourage you to seek the help and advice you need. Talk with your husband, partner, or best friends. Talk to your sisters, brothers, or parents. Have them read this book too so they can get an idea of what you are going through.

Once you have told the first person, things will get easier. Don't stop and don't lose the momentum. I don't want you to get into even one more PMDD luteal phase of your cycle before getting help. Search for a "reproductive psychiatrist near me". This is a very specialized field that is continuing to grow, so if there are none near you, then start with any psychologist, psychiatrist, or therapist you can get in to see in the next week. Join the IAPMD FaceBook support groups. Start following people on Instagram who are advocating for women's health. Be proactive and start to record and track your symptoms and moods (at the back of this book). My prayer is that you gain the confidence and strength you need to advocate for yourself until you find the best healing for you, your relationships, and your overall well being. You deserve it, so "Keep Calm and *Do No Harm*."

Acknowledgements

I thank God for helping me walk through the shadows and come out stronger on the other side. He was with me the whole time (every month)... and He was also there for my husband and kids when I wasn't present. Thank you, Lord.

I wrote this book to save lives, but it would not have been possible if I did not have people in my corner rooting for me first to get better myself. Thank you to my husband Jade for sticking with me even when my crazy was on full display. Your even keel and peaceful demeanor helped me through the toughest of days. Thank you for being there for our kids when I wasn't.

My children are at a young age so as I continue to heal and get better, I am hoping that means they will forget how their mom was not always present for them. If they do remember, then I hope they can learn from me that it is okay to not be okay, as long as you make moves to get better. I am so grateful that God chose me to be their mother and despite this rough journey, I would not have it any other way.

My parents, sisters, and brother were phenomenal when it came to supporting and encouraging me. They didn't judge when I told them about PMDD. They were fully engaged in my healing process and furthermore became some of my biggest fans when I told them I was going to write a book about my experiences.

Thank you to my grandmother Ganny, who supported my dream in many ways and believed in me before I believed in myself.

Thank you to Ed and Francine for making such a wonderful human being in your son Jade.

To my #6BFFs, #BoyMoms, and #HoodieGang, thank you for always being there for me. You are all mothers and didn't bat an eye when I would confide in you about my despair. You offered ideas to help me without judgment. You planned multiple girls' weekends so I could have much needed breaks. Thank you.

My teacher neighbors in the 800 Hallway, 500 Hallway, and 600 Hallway got me through many days of teaching when I wasn't on point, and I am so grateful to have you in my life. In particular, thank you to my 600 Hallway peeps who had a front row seat to my PMDD struggles and still had my back. "But Have You Read the Book?" Book Club, thank you for giving me an escape with the RomComs we would read.

To Keeth Matheny aka Coach Rudy (author of *ExSELent Teaching*) and the School-Connect® team, thank you for making such an amazing curriculum that had the impact of saving not only countless lives of teenagers, but my life, too. You are doing a great thing. Keep it up!

Thank you to Dan Dillard of FoundingAustin and Nest Financial for giving me the platform to first write for the masses.

Thank you to my neighbor Cat for being my first sounding board and for the priceless advice. Thank you to Mrs. Fuller for listening to me during our coffee dates while I brainstormed how to make the book better. Thank you to Sarah Robb and Dr. Adrienne Kennedy for your feedback on the very early drafts.

This book would have taken forever to get on the shelves if it weren't for the help of my trusted advisors. My cousin Adam Peyton (Author of The Adventures of Daisy and Buster: A Kolache in Karachi) walked me through the steps of self-publishing. My cousin Audrey Bushfield Kidd explained the ins and outs of the publishing world and advised me on building my platform. Lauren Daly (author of *Sorry, I Spaced Out...* and *Rosa's Feelings*) guided me in the self-publication process. P.A. Spence (author of *Beneath the Sweet Magnolias*) (*"Tales from the Dirt Hills"*) edited, walked me through the self-publication process, edited, mentored, encouraged, and edited again. Thank you for being my writing partner, Patty!

To all the women out there who have PMDD and still fight to get better, fight to be yourselves, and fight for your relationships, you all are my heroes. You are doing a great thing by paving the way. I hope you continue to "Keep Calm and *Do No Harm*".

References

American Psychiatric Association. (2013). *Diagnostic and Statistical Manual of Mental Disorders* (5th ed.).

American Psychiatric Association. (1994). *Diagnostic and Statistical Manual of Mental Disorders* (4th ed.).

American Psychiatric Association. (1987). Diagnostic and Statistical Manual of Mental Disorders (3rd ed., revised).

Baylor College of Medicine Reproductive Psychiatry -

https://www.bcm.edu/healthcare/specialties/obstetrics-and-gynecology/reproductive-psychiatry

Bilodeau, Kelly. "Managing Intrusive Thoughts", Harvard Health Publishing, October 1, 2021.

https://www.health.harvard.edu/mind-and-mood/managing-intrusive-thoughts

Church Unlimited

https://churchunlimited.com/

Cowan, Beryl Ann. "Incarcerated women: Poverty, trauma and unmet need", *The SES Indicator,* April 2019.

https://www.apa.org/pi/ses/resources/indicator/2019/04/inc arcerated-women

Das, Sneha. "Spain becomes the first European country to approve menstrual leave." *NewsBytes,* February 17, 2023.

https://www.newsbytesapp.com/news/world/spain-approves-menstrual-leave/story#:~:text=On%20Thursday%2C%20in%20a%20historic%20move%2C%20Spain%20became,by%20185%20votes%20in%20favor%20to%20154%20against.

Dubey, N et al. "The ESC/E(Z) complex, an effector of response to ovarian steroids, manifests an intrinsic difference in cells from women with premenstrual dysphoric disorder." *Molecular psychiatry* vol. 22,8 (2017): 1172-1184. doi:10.1038/mp.2016.229

Dweck, Carol S. "The Power of Yet", TEDx Norrköping. September 12, 2014.

https://www.youtube.com/watch?v=J-swZaKN2Ic

Endicott, Jean. "History, Evolution, and Diagnosis of Premenstrual Dysphoric Disorder" *Journal of Clinical Psychiatry* (2000;61[suppl 12]:5-8).

"Fact Sheet: Women & Socioeconomic Status". *American Psychological Association.*

https://www.apa.org/pi/ses/resources/publications/women

Frankl, Viktor E. (Viktor Emil), 1905-1997 author. *Man's Search for Meaning : An Introduction to Logotherapy.* Boston :Beacon Press, 1962.

Goggins, David. *Never Finished: Unshackle Your Mind and Win the War Within.* Lionscrest Publishing, 2022.

Guarnotta, Emily and Mona Bapat. "7 Examples of Intrusive Thoughts (and What You Can Do About Them)", GoodRx Health, April 11, 2023.

https://www.goodrx.com/conditions/obsessive-compulsive-disorder/intrusive-thoughts-examples

Henley, William Ernest. "Invictus." *Poetry Foundation*, Poetry Foundation, 2023,

https://www.poetryfoundation.org/poems/51642/invictus.

International Association for Premenstrual Disorders (IAPMD)

https://iapmd.org/

IAPMD - PMDD Moms Support Group on FaceBook

IAPMD - PMDD, Oophorectomy, Hysterectomy, & Life After Group on FaceBook

International Classification of Diseases, Eleventh Revision (ICD-11), World Health Organization (WHO) 2019/2021

https://icd.who.int/browse11 .

Licensed under Creative Commons Attribution-NoDerivatives 3.0 IGO license (CC BY-ND 3.0 IGO).

Jones, Heather M. "PMDD Almost Ruined My Life Before I Found out What It Was." *Parents Magazine,* February 7, 2020, https://www.parents.com/parenting/moms/healthy-mom/pmdd-almost-ruined-my-life/

Lewis, N. Alysha. "The Real Reasons Women of Color Lack Access to Health Care", *SheKnows*, February 10, 2023.

https://www.sheknows.com/health-and-wellness/articles/2002411/women-of-color-health-care/

Longfellow, Henry Wadsworth. "There Was a Little Girl." *Poetry Foundation*, Poetry Foundation, 2021,

www.poetryfoundation.org/poems/44650/there-was-a-little-girl

Marusic, Kristina. "The Sickening Truth About What It's Like to Get Your Period in Prison: A look into the cruel and disturbing ways female prisoners must deal with their menstrual health." *Women's Health Magazine*. July 7, 2016.

https://www.womenshealthmag.com/life/a19997775/women-jail-periods/

Matheny, R. Keeth. *ExSELent Teaching: Classroom strategies to support the social, emotional, and academic growth of students*. Paperback – January 31, 2022.

"More Than Able" (feat. Chandler Moore & Tiffany Hudson) | Elevation Worship: *Can You Imagine?* (2023)

https://youtu.be/dQ1xxoP7NJk

"New International Version" 2023. *The Holy Bible*. Zondervan.

Ogletree, Kelsey. *"Women Were Left Out of Clinical Trials Until the '90s—This Is How It's Impacted Our Health." Well and Good*, July 6, 2020.

https://www.wellandgood.com/women-clinical-trials/#What%20Are%20The%20Problems%20Created%20Ofrom%20Omitting%20Women%20from%20Clinical%20Trials?

Population of the United States by sex and age as of July 1, 2021.

https://www.statista.com/statistics/241488/population-of-the-us-by-sex-and-age/

"Premenstrual dysphoria disorder: It's biology, not a behavior choice". *Harvard Health Blog*, May 30, 2017.

https://www.health.harvard.edu/blog/premenstrual-dysphoria-disorder-its-biology-not-a-behavior-choice-2017053011768

Prisoners Series (1980-2021). Washington, DC.

Raffi, Edwin R. and Marlene P. Freeman. "The etiology of premenstrual dysphoric disorder: 5 interwoven pieces." *Current Psychiatry.* (2017) September;16(9):20-28.

Ro, Christine. "The overlooked condition that can trigger extreme behaviour." BBC Future, December 15, 2019.

https://www.bbc.com/future/article/20191213-pmdd-a-little-understood-and-often-misdiagnosed-condition

School-Connect®

https://school-connect.net/

"Sex hormone-sensitive gene complex linked to premenstrual mood disorder - Dysregulated cellular response to estrogen and progesterone suspected." *National Institutes of Health.* January 3, 2017 News Release.

https://www.nih.gov/news-events/news-releases/sex-hormone-sensitive-gene-complex-linked-premenstrual-mood-disorder

Simon, B. (1978). *Mind and madness in ancient Greece: The classical roots of modern psychiatry.* Cornell U Press.

Stiernman, L., Dubol, M., Comasco, E. *et al.* Emotion-induced brain activation across the menstrual cycle in individuals with premenstrual dysphoric disorder and associations to serum levels of progesterone-derived neurosteroids. *Transl Psychiatry* 13, 124 (2023). https://doi.org/10.1038/s41398-023-02424-3

The Johns Hopkins Reproductive Mental Health Center

https://www.hopkinsmedicine.org/psychiatry/specialty_areas/moods/clinic_rmh.html

The Massachusetts General Hospital Center for Women's Mental Health.

https://womensmentalhealth.org/

The Mayo Clinic

https://www.mayoclinic.org/departments-centers/womens-health

YouVersion Bible App –

https://www.youversion.com/the-bible-app/

World Health Organization –

https://www.who.int/

Tracking Your Symptoms

Please use the following charts to track your symptoms. Check to see how they align with your cycle. Advocate for yourself! You got this!

January

Symptoms and Moods	1	2	3	4	5	6	7	8	9	10	11	12	13	14
Markedly depressed mood, feelings of hopelessness, or self-deprecating thoughts.														
Marked anxiety, tension, feelings of being "keyed up" or "on edge".														
Marked affective lability (e.g., mood swings, feeling suddenly sad or tearful, or increased sensitivity to rejection).														
Marked irritability or anger or increased interpersonal conflicts.														
Decreased interest in usual activities (e.g., work, school, friends, hobbies).														
Subjective difficulty in concentration.														
Lethargy, easy fatigability, or marked lack of energy.														
Marked change in appetite; overeating; or specific food cravings.														
Hypersomnia or insomnia.														
A sense of being overwhelmed or out of control.														
Physical symptoms such as breast tenderness or swelling, joint or muscle pain, a sensation of "bloating", or weight gain.														

15	16	17	18	19	20	21	22	23	24	25	26	27	28	29	30

NOTES FOR THE MONTH:

NOTES FOR THE MONTH:

February

Symptoms and Moods	1	2	3	4	5	6	7	8	9	10	11	12	13	14
Markedly depressed mood, feelings of hopelessness, or self-deprecating thoughts.														
Marked anxiety, tension, feelings of being "keyed up" or "on edge".														
Marked affective lability (e.g., mood swings, feeling suddenly sad or tearful, or increased sensitivity to rejection).														
Marked irritability or anger or increased interpersonal conflicts.														
Decreased interest in usual activities (e.g., work, school, friends, hobbies).														
Subjective difficulty in concentration.														
Lethargy, easy fatigability, or marked lack of energy.														
Marked change in appetite; overeating; or specific food cravings.														
Hypersomnia or insomnia.														
A sense of being overwhelmed or out of control.														
Physical symptoms such as breast tenderness or swelling, joint or muscle pain, a sensation of "bloating", or weight gain.														

15	16	17	18	19	20	21	22	23	24	25	26	27	28	29	30

NOTES FOR THE MONTH:

NOTES FOR THE MONTH:

March

Symptoms and Moods	1	2	3	4	5	6	7	8	9	10	11	12	13	14
Markedly depressed mood, feelings of hopelessness, or self-deprecating thoughts.														
Marked anxiety, tension, feelings of being "keyed up" or "on edge".														
Marked affective lability (e.g., mood swings, feeling suddenly sad or tearful, or increased sensitivity to rejection).														
Marked irritability or anger or increased interpersonal conflicts.														
Decreased interest in usual activities (e.g., work, school, friends, hobbies).														
Subjective difficulty in concentration.														
Lethargy, easy fatigability, or marked lack of energy.														
Marked change in appetite; overeating; or specific food cravings.														
Hypersomnia or insomnia.														
A sense of being overwhelmed or out of control.														
Physical symptoms such as breast tenderness or swelling, joint or muscle pain, a sensation of "bloating", or weight gain.														

15	16	17	18	19	20	21	22	23	24	25	26	27	28	29	30

NOTES FOR THE MONTH:

NOTES FOR THE MONTH:

April

Symptoms and Moods	1	2	3	4	5	6	7	8	9	10	11	12	13	14
Markedly depressed mood, feelings of hopelessness, or self-deprecating thoughts.														
Marked anxiety, tension, feelings of being "keyed up" or "on edge".														
Marked affective lability (e.g., mood swings, feeling suddenly sad or tearful, or increased sensitivity to rejection).														
Marked irritability or anger or increased interpersonal conflicts.														
Decreased interest in usual activities (e.g., work, school, friends, hobbies).														
Subjective difficulty in concentration.														
Lethargy, easy fatigability, or marked lack of energy.														
Marked change in appetite; overeating; or specific food cravings.														
Hypersomnia or insomnia.														
A sense of being overwhelmed or out of control.														
Physical symptoms such as breast tenderness or swelling, joint or muscle pain, a sensation of "bloating", or weight gain.														

15	16	17	18	19	20	21	22	23	24	25	26	27	28	29	30

NOTES FOR THE MONTH:

NOTES FOR THE MONTH:

May

Symptoms and Moods	1	2	3	4	5	6	7	8	9	10	11	12	13	14
Markedly depressed mood, feelings of hopelessness, or self-deprecating thoughts.														
Marked anxiety, tension, feelings of being "keyed up" or "on edge".														
Marked affective lability (e.g., mood swings, feeling suddenly sad or tearful, or increased sensitivity to rejection).														
Marked irritability or anger or increased interpersonal conflicts.														
Decreased interest in usual activities (e.g., work, school, friends, hobbies).														
Subjective difficulty in concentration.														
Lethargy, easy fatigability, or marked lack of energy.														
Marked change in appetite; overeating; or specific food cravings.														
Hypersomnia or insomnia.														
A sense of being overwhelmed or out of control.														
Physical symptoms such as breast tenderness or swelling, joint or muscle pain, a sensation of "bloating", or weight gain.														

15	16	17	18	19	20	21	22	23	24	25	26	27	28	29	30

NOTES FOR THE MONTH:

NOTES FOR THE MONTH:

June

Symptoms and Moods	1	2	3	4	5	6	7	8	9	10	11	12	13	14
Markedly depressed mood, feelings of hopelessness, or self-deprecating thoughts.														
Marked anxiety, tension, feelings of being "keyed up" or "on edge".														
Marked affective lability (e.g., mood swings, feeling suddenly sad or tearful, or increased sensitivity to rejection).														
Marked irritability or anger or increased interpersonal conflicts.														
Decreased interest in usual activities (e.g., work, school, friends, hobbies).														
Subjective difficulty in concentration.														
Lethargy, easy fatigability, or marked lack of energy.														
Marked change in appetite; overeating; or specific food cravings.														
Hypersomnia or insomnia.														
A sense of being overwhelmed or out of control.														
Physical symptoms such as breast tenderness or swelling, joint or muscle pain, a sensation of "bloating", or weight gain.														

15	16	17	18	19	20	21	22	23	24	25	26	27	28	29	30

143

NOTES FOR THE MONTH:

NOTES FOR THE MONTH:

July

Symptoms and Moods	1	2	3	4	5	6	7	8	9	10	11	12	13	14
Markedly depressed mood, feelings of hopelessness, or self-deprecating thoughts.														
Marked anxiety, tension, feelings of being "keyed up" or "on edge".														
Marked affective lability (e.g., mood swings, feeling suddenly sad or tearful, or increased sensitivity to rejection).														
Marked irritability or anger or increased interpersonal conflicts.														
Decreased interest in usual activities (e.g., work, school, friends, hobbies).														
Subjective difficulty in concentration.														
Lethargy, easy fatigability, or marked lack of energy.														
Marked change in appetite; overeating; or specific food cravings.														
Hypersomnia or insomnia.														
A sense of being overwhelmed or out of control.														
Physical symptoms such as breast tenderness or swelling, joint or muscle pain, a sensation of "bloating", or weight gain.														

15	16	17	18	19	20	21	22	23	24	25	26	27	28	29	30

NOTES FOR THE MONTH:

NOTES FOR THE MONTH:

August

Symptoms and Moods	1	2	3	4	5	6	7	8	9	10	11	12	13	14
Markedly depressed mood, feelings of hopelessness, or self-deprecating thoughts.														
Marked anxiety, tension, feelings of being "keyed up" or "on edge".														
Marked affective lability (e.g., mood swings, feeling suddenly sad or tearful, or increased sensitivity to rejection).														
Marked irritability or anger or increased interpersonal conflicts.														
Decreased interest in usual activities (e.g., work, school, friends, hobbies).														
Subjective difficulty in concentration.														
Lethargy, easy fatigability, or marked lack of energy.														
Marked change in appetite; overeating; or specific food cravings.														
Hypersomnia or insomnia.														
A sense of being overwhelmed or out of control.														
Physical symptoms such as breast tenderness or swelling, joint or muscle pain, a sensation of "bloating", or weight gain.														

15	16	17	18	19	20	21	22	23	24	25	26	27	28	29	30

NOTES FOR THE MONTH:

NOTES FOR THE MONTH:

September

Symptoms and Moods	1	2	3	4	5	6	7	8	9	10	11	12	13	14
Markedly depressed mood, feelings of hopelessness, or self-deprecating thoughts.														
Marked anxiety, tension, feelings of being "keyed up" or "on edge".														
Marked affective lability (e.g., mood swings, feeling suddenly sad or tearful, or increased sensitivity to rejection).														
Marked irritability or anger or increased interpersonal conflicts.														
Decreased interest in usual activities (e.g., work, school, friends, hobbies).														
Subjective difficulty in concentration.														
Lethargy, easy fatigability, or marked lack of energy.														
Marked change in appetite; overeating; or specific food cravings.														
Hypersomnia or insomnia.														
A sense of being overwhelmed or out of control.														
Physical symptoms such as breast tenderness or swelling, joint or muscle pain, a sensation of "bloating", or weight gain.														

15	16	17	18	19	20	21	22	23	24	25	26	27	28	29	30

NOTES FOR THE MONTH:

NOTES FOR THE MONTH:

October

Symptoms and Moods	1	2	3	4	5	6	7	8	9	10	11	12	13	14
Markedly depressed mood, feelings of hopelessness, or self-deprecating thoughts.														
Marked anxiety, tension, feelings of being "keyed up" or "on edge".														
Marked affective lability (e.g., mood swings, feeling suddenly sad or tearful, or increased sensitivity to rejection).														
Marked irritability or anger or increased interpersonal conflicts.														
Decreased interest in usual activities (e.g., work, school, friends, hobbies).														
Subjective difficulty in concentration.														
Lethargy, easy fatigability, or marked lack of energy.														
Marked change in appetite; overeating; or specific food cravings.														
Hypersomnia or insomnia.														
A sense of being overwhelmed or out of control.														
Physical symptoms such as breast tenderness or swelling, joint or muscle pain, a sensation of "bloating", or weight gain.														

15	16	17	18	19	20	21	22	23	24	25	26	27	28	29	30

NOTES FOR THE MONTH:

NOTES FOR THE MONTH:

November

Symptoms and Moods	1	2	3	4	5	6	7	8	9	10	11	12	13	14
Markedly depressed mood, feelings of hopelessness, or self-deprecating thoughts.														
Marked anxiety, tension, feelings of being "keyed up" or "on edge".														
Marked affective lability (e.g., mood swings, feeling suddenly sad or tearful, or increased sensitivity to rejection).														
Marked irritability or anger or increased interpersonal conflicts.														
Decreased interest in usual activities (e.g., work, school, friends, hobbies).														
Subjective difficulty in concentration.														
Lethargy, easy fatigability, or marked lack of energy.														
Marked change in appetite; overeating; or specific food cravings.														
Hypersomnia or insomnia.														
A sense of being overwhelmed or out of control.														
Physical symptoms such as breast tenderness or swelling, joint or muscle pain, a sensation of "bloating", or weight gain.														

15	16	17	18	19	20	21	22	23	24	25	26	27	28	29	30

NOTES FOR THE MONTH:

NOTES FOR THE MONTH:

December

Symptoms and Moods	1	2	3	4	5	6	7	8	9	10	11	12	13	14
Markedly depressed mood, feelings of hopelessness, or self-deprecating thoughts.														
Marked anxiety, tension, feelings of being "keyed up" or "on edge".														
Marked affective lability (e.g., mood swings, feeling suddenly sad or tearful, or increased sensitivity to rejection).														
Marked irritability or anger or increased interpersonal conflicts.														
Decreased interest in usual activities (e.g., work, school, friends, hobbies).														
Subjective difficulty in concentration.														
Lethargy, easy fatigability, or marked lack of energy.														
Marked change in appetite; overeating; or specific food cravings.														
Hypersomnia or insomnia.														
A sense of being overwhelmed or out of control.														
Physical symptoms such as breast tenderness or swelling, joint or muscle pain, a sensation of "bloating", or weight gain.														

15	16	17	18	19	20	21	22	23	24	25	26	27	28	29	30

NOTES FOR THE MONTH:

NOTES FOR THE MONTH:

About the Author

Candace Peyton Wofford is a UT Longhorn and cheese connoisseur. She grew up in Austin, Texas, and now lives in Corpus Christi, Texas with her husband Jade and their two kids. Now that her health is back on track, in addition to running around with her kids, you can find Candace enjoying a rom-com book at the beach, catching up on shows, or experimenting with colorful foods in the kitchen.

candacepeytonwofford.com

candacepeytonwofford

candacepeytonwofford

Made in the USA
Middletown, DE
19 October 2023

41078820R00099